HOW TO
Get Your Kids
to Clean
Their Rooms
AND OTHER IMPOSSIBLE TASKS

HOW TO

Get Your Kids to Clean Their Rooms

AND OTHER IMPOSSIBLE TASKS

WAYS TO HELP A CHILD BE MORE RESPONSIBLE

The Parenting Resource Group
with Dr. Henry Isaksen

S & B Publishers   Woodland Hills, Utah 84653

The Parenting Resource Group is composed of parents, educators, and child development professionals who work together to compile easy-to-read helps for parents. Dr. Henry Isaksen, educator and family counselor, represents the group as primary spokesman on this book.

Copyright © 1982 by Hanks/Belliston Associates

All rights reserved. No part of this book may be reproduced or used in any form or by any means—graphic, electronic, or mechanical; photocopying, recording, or information storage or retrieval system—without written permission of the publisher.

Printed in the United States of America.

In cooperation with The Parenting Resource Group, this book was prepared through the joint efforts of: Larry Belliston, Producer/Director; Kurt Hanks, Director; Jay A. Parry, Editor; Richard Moore, Research; Marge Neuharth, Art Production; Becky Miller, Illustrator.

Contents

Why This Book Can Make a Difference

Whoever said raising kids was easy was never a parent! See if any of these sounds familiar to you:

John won't clean his room
Rebecca keeps forgetting to feed her cat

Trudy and Mac are always fighting
Rob doesn't like to make his bed
Jan hates to brush her teeth

Getting Steve to practice on the piano is like *pulling* teeth!
Melanie never does her homework

1

Have any of those things ever happened at your house? And you've wondered what to do, right?

We've been faced with the same challenges with our children. That's how this book came to be: a need for meaningful answers. We reviewed what the professional-experts had to say. We talked to parent-experts. One answer kept coming up again and again.

Every situation in every home is different, of course. Only the parent who's in the thick of it can decide what's best in a particular set of circumstances. **But there is one thing that will make a difference in almost every situation: help the child become more responsible.** The child who has developed the skill and character trait of responsibility will be more likely to do his chores, brush his teeth, get along with his sister, obey his mother—and do on his own all the other things that need to be done.

It seems almost that responsibility is a magic wand that will get rid of all our troubles. And, surprisingly enough, it almost is! It's not magic, of course. But it *can* make a world of difference to the home.

How can a parent wave this magic wand and get all of the benefits it offers? This book will give you dozens of ways. But don't think you have to follow all the suggestions. Read through the book, get the ideas, and then apply them as needed. One will work here, one there. You may want to use one idea today, another tomorrow. Then come back to the book and get more ideas. Mark it up. Jot notes in the margins. *Use* it!

A child doesn't become responsible in just a day. It takes time. But this book will give you some tips you can apply now, today, that will help the child to *act* responsibly even before he or she has really acquired the trait. There are ideas here that can help you with immediate problems. But it will also help you develop your child over the long term. Both benefits are very real. And both are simple and easy to achieve.

How do you get a child to clean his room and other impossible tasks? Teach him to be responsible, and you won't have to GET him to do anything. When he's responsible, he'll be self-motivated. And then he'll do it on his own!

Why Nagging Doesn't Teach Responsibility

"You're such a little slob. Why can't you clean up after yourself? Who taught you to be such a pig? Start to do better. If you don't you'll be sorry. Blah, blah, blah, blah."

Mack is supposed to clean up the table after supper. Everyone else in the family has left the room. He diddles and dawdles and still doesn't get it done. Finally mother comes in. "You're so slow. Get busy."

He diddles and dawdles some more. Mom comes in again. "You'd better hurry up or I'm going to spank you!"

Mack diddles.

"All right, you little brat! That's enough!" And mom descends like an eagle from her nest, claws outstretched!

Mack and his mom are in a rut. He's supposed to do something and doesn't do it. His mom nags, then punishes. It's a vicious, endless cycle. Mack never learns any responsibility. And his mom never gets the work done.

In helping children learn to be responsible, it works best to emphasize the positive and deemphasize the negative. Don't dwell on what they're doing wrong. Dwell on what they're doing right.

Be Positive for Lasting Results

The positive approach always works best. Oh, the negative sometimes gets immediate results (only sometimes!). But long-term results come only from emphasizing the positive.

- Tell the child what he can do, not what he can't.
- Give the child support, not criticism.
- Make life enjoyable for the child, not miserable.
- Practice being more aware of the positive actions of a child.
- Reward for positive behavior. And realize that punishment is also a form of reward—a form that's to be avoided.

Once they start looking for the positive, parents may be surprised at how much the child does *right*! Then the parents can respond by talking and acting positively, which will reinforce the good things the child is doing.

What's a Parent to Do?

Here are some ideas that will help a parent emphasize the positive:

1. *Tone of voice can convey respect for the child.* It can show the child that his parent values him as a unique person. Solomon said, "A soft answer turneth away wrath." Oftentimes how you say something is more important than what you say.

2. *What a child learns, he lives.* Melanie hears criticism all day. She starts to believe it. Before long she things she isn't worth much—if she were, her parents would know about it, wouldn't they? Bess hears more positive things. She begins to believe what she hears. She must be a valuable person. Her parents wouldn't treat her that way if she weren't.

4

3. *Insults, name-calling, and threats are always counterproductive.* "Rusty, you're just a brat. You're so messy. You can't do anything right." It all becomes a self-fulfilling prophecy. Rusty starts to act more and more like a brat. He gets more and more messy, klutzier and klutzier. Why? Because that's how his parents said he was. Avoid these, because they're all destructive: insults, name-calling, threats, bossing, predictions of failure. Predict failure in a child and he'll prove you right.

4. *Praising responsible behavior causes the child to repeat it.* When Steve does a good job of cleaning his room, say so. When Marsha is quick to do her job of raking the leaves, praise her for her work. When Jeff calls you because he's going to be late getting home from school, thank him for being so thoughtful. The more a parent praises his kids for being responsible, the more the kids will want to be responsible.

5. *The parent who is quick to respond to accomplishments is the parent who is building a responsible child.* The parent who is slow to anger is the parent who is giving his child room to grow.

6. *Giving misbehavior more attention than good behavior will be counterproductive.* Rather than getting the child to change, it will cause him to seek more of your attention—and that comes from misbehaving more. Jenny never did her homework. Her grades dropped. And so did her relationship with her parents, as they nagged and nagged, giving her lack of responsibility all kinds of attention. But when they focused on the things she was doing right, she suddenly started to do better with her homework. The rewards came only for the things she was doing well, and she wanted to get more rewards.

Once a parent gets started on the positive approach, things will begin to improve. But improvement may not come immediately. It may take time for the parent to switch from a punishing, nagging approach. It may take the children time to make adjustments to a new kind of parent, too! But once the nagging and negativism are gone, the child will begin to respond. And life will be easier (and more productive) for everyone!

Why Most Kids Aren't Responsible

If a child doesn't know *how* to be responsible, he won't be able to behave the way his parents would like him to. And about the only way he'll be able to learn is if the parents take the time to teach him.

Teaching is a critical part of a parent-child relationship. The parent knows much from experience that he'd like to share with his child. The child knows the parent is bigger and stronger and often smarter than he is. And the child looks to the parent for instruction and example in how he should be.

If the child isn't taught how to be responsible, he probably won't ever learn. Responsibility is a skill as well as an attitude. It must be learned just as a person learns how to drive a car or fly an airplane.

Rob worked at an airport as a clean-up boy. One day he started bragging to his friends that he could fly. "Yeah," he said. "I took lessons last summer and now I fly all the time."

The friends weren't too sure they believed him. "You've never mentioned this before. If you really can fly, why didn't you say something sooner?"

Before long Rob was backed into a corner. He either had to put up or shut up. So he agreed to take a couple of friends up for a ride. He took them to a plane that belonged to a businessman in the area. "It's okay. He lets me fly it anytime I want." They climbed in, and Rob took off. So far, so good. It's not that hard to get up plane off the ground.

But once he was up, he didn't know what to do. And landing is much harder than taking off.

The control tower talked Rob and his friends down. He wrecked the plane in the process.

Working around airplanes doesn't make a person a pilot. Living around responsible people doesn't make a person responsible. The skill must be practiced to be acquired.

Hauling Hay

A fellow named Jason tells this story: "I was unloading hay as a teenager, and I'd worked hard all day at the job. We'd unload a semi-truckload and hardly have time to breathe before another one came in. When quitting time came, the farmer told us to go on home. But he warned us that another truck might be coming in. If it arrived, he'd give us a call.

"I dragged myself home and promptly took the phone off the hook. I didn't want to have to worry about going back out to work that night.

"When my dad got home from work he asked why the phone was off the hook. I told him. And he told me to get my rear in gear and get back out to the farmer's. When I arrived, the farmer and the other boys were in the middle of the last truckload. I helped until the job was done.

"At the time I was ticked off at my dad for making me go back out there. But I know now he was making the effort to teach me a little more about being responsible."

A child will learn about his world in one way or another. If the parent doesn't teach him, someone else will. And what if that other person doesn't teach the right things? What if the child learns to drive on the wrong side of the road? Or what if he starts to think he can fly when he really can't?

A child won't know to put her toys away unless she's taught to do so. The same is true of every other form of responsibility.

7

What's a Parent to Do?

The best way to help a child learn how to be responsible is to teach him, little by little, day by day. As we teach our children, we should keep these points in mind:

- If we try to teach when the child is tired or hungry or upset, we'll almost certainly fail. Poor timing is a frequent cause of ineffective learning.

- We shouldn't try to teach when there's a time limit involved. Pressure causes both parent and child to get upset, and the teaching situation is ruined.

- Criticism is a poison when combined with teaching. The two go together like sand and gas in a car engine.

- We need to be patient. It takes time for anyone to change his ways, to grow and develop, and children are no different.

When to Start Teaching Responsibility

Coaches start out right with their players on the first day of practice. Parents should start out teaching responsibility to their kids from the very first.

Ned was thirteen and a real brat. He would never do as he was told; he wouldn't ever help around the house on his own; he sassed his parents and tormented his brothers and sisters.

Ned's room was always a mess. If it got cleaned, his mother had to do it.

He wouldn't put his dirty clothes in the hamper where they belonged. Instead he'd kick them under the bed or drop them in the closet. Then he'd bawl his mother out when he didn't have any clothes to wear.

He got a nice allowance every week, but it was gone the next day. Then he'd go begging to his dad for more money. Usually he got it, after a fight.

When Ned was 13½, his dad decided to take matters in hand. Ned's irresponsibility had gone on for too long. He dad put him on notice: "We've had enough, Ned," dad said as kindly as he could. "You need to change and we're going to help you."

Dad had good intentions—but Ned was stronger than dad was. Ned put up resistance longer than dad could take it. Finally dad gave up, totally frustrated.

The longer we wait before teaching responsibility, the harder it generally is. That's not to say that Ned's dad couldn't have done it successfully. But the longer the parents wait, the more the child will become stuck in his ways. And it will take a lot more energy to dislodge him.

The sooner you start with your child, the easier it will be to teach him to be responsible. And the more effective.

Develop Them in One Area

"After struggling with toilet-training through three kids, I finally found a way that works! The method is so simple, I wonder why I didn't think of it sooner. And the neat thing is that it teaches *all* the children to be more responsible. It works because the kids are young enough to get excited about it.

"Here's how it works. When the baby is ready to toilet train, I get all of the kids together. I tell them I want them to help me train the baby. Whenever the baby successfully uses the toilet, I explain, each of the children will get a treat.

"Instantly all the children pitch in and help. They encourage, cajole, demonstrate—anything to help the baby learn to use the toilet instead of his pants.

"My method works! And while it's teaching the baby to use the toilet, it's also teaching all the other kids to be responsible in helping the baby.

"If my children were older, they wouldn't be so interested in helping. But they're young—I started early—and they're excited to have the responsibility of helping. The things the children are learning in that one instance carry over into other parts of their lives. They transfer the pattern of responsibility into other areas.

"I've really noticed how willing little kids are to help. They *want* to be responsible. they *want* to learn how to be like mommy or daddy. All they need is a little guidance and a little patience while they're learning."

Marge Belliston

What's a Parent to Do?

The earlier you can start with your child, the better. An infant shouldn't be expected to be responsible in any way, of course. But as soon as your baby learns to understand spoken language (which occurs sometime before she can speak herself), you can begin the training in responsibility. Most parents make the mistake of waiting too long.

Start in little ways. Set a few rules, such as what the child can get into and what she can't, and stick with them. Be loving, but firm. "No, Nancy, you're not to get into the books."

She won't understand it much at first, and she'll take constant monitoring. But, little by little, you'll be teaching her that life has limits, and that things work out better when we stay within them.

When she's big enough to walk, she can pick up her toys.

When she's three or four, you can have her make her bed.

When she's five or six, she can set the table.

When she's seven or eight, she can play at a friend's house and be responsible for getting home on time.

Kids can accept responsibility quite early. They're not too young at five or six to set the table—and they can do it even earlier with some help.

Little by little, you'll be teaching her that responsibility is an important part of life. She won't learn all at once. She'll have setbacks. But as you consistently teach her, she'll develop her own responsibility.

Now, what if you're reading this now and some or all of your children are a little older? What can you do?

Don't despair! Chances are you've been teaching your child much about being responsible without even thinking about it. For example, you've probably had her doing chores around the house. When she goes out, you probably require her to be back at a certain time. You almost certainly expect her to be truthful and honest with you.

So it's not as though you're starting at point zero. You've moved up the responsibility scale without even meaning to.

How does a parent move ahead with his or her older child? The principles for teaching responsibility are the same no matter what the age of the child. Just don't expect any overnight miracles. Start with little things. Let the child develop in areas she can. Then move on to other facets of responsibility. Even an adult who's had no experience with being responsible can learn to do better. But he has to start small.

And the sooner you get your child going, the better!

Kids will often learn responsibility simply by mimicking their parents. A good example is crucial, at every age!

How Much Responsibility Do You Give?

One day Rod wasn't behaving up to his mother's expectations. He was being a little silly when she wanted to be serious. She got angry. "You're acting like a sixteen-year-old," she said, intending the ultimate insult.

Rod had the perfect comeback. "But mom—I *am* sixteen!"

Different people have different capacities for being responsible. The same child has different capacities at different times. The ability to be responsible can be affected by

- age
- experience
- intelligence
- aptitude

- training
- needs
- desires
- maturity

- education
- values
- emotions
- health

13

A child will be able to respond only if his capacity fits the responsibility that's being required of him.

Too Much or Too little

There is a danger in giving too much responsibility too soon—but there's also a danger in giving too little too late.

Too much too soon leads to failure. Ask your child to water the lawn. If he's too young for the task, he'll fail. If he'd punished for failing, the problem will grow worse. If the responsibility is taken away, he'll feel like he let you down. He'll feel unworthy as a person.

Failure isn't the end of the world. Every child can handle a few such failures. But a constant diet of it will ruin him. He'll end up feeling incompetent. And incompetent people have trouble with responsibility throughout their lives.

If your child is old enough, have him water the lawn. That means he turns on the tap when you tell him to. As he grows older, you can let him choose where to place the sprinkler. And when he's older still, he can decide when the lawn needs watering.

Another approach is to let the child do the whole thing. But supervise closely as he develops his capacity for the responsibility. Over the months that follow, as the child learns the job, you can gradually withdraw supervision. The effect will be that his responsibility increases—but he probably won't even notice.

What's a Parent to Do?

In helping your child grow, remember this: Giving responsibility is like having a child carry a load. The weight of the load will depend on the capacity of the child. A baby can carry almost no load at all. A teenager may be able to carry 50 to 100 pounds. A kid in between will be able to carry a load that matches his size and strength.

Overload the child and you'll crush him with the weight. Underload him and he'll never develop his muscles. But give him just the right weight and you'll be raising a responsible kid. And his responsibility muscles will grow stronger as they're exercised more and more.

A Starting Point to Building Responsibility

Weakness is inevitable in any child (and adult!). There's no such thing as a perfectly rounded person—and when you emphasize one area of your life, you'll end up *de*emphasizing another area. It's a law of existence.

And what happens? The person develops some real strengths, some mountains of ability; but at the same time, in contrast, he's perpetuating some weaknesses, which are valleys beside his mountains.

In teaching children responsibility, we have two choices:

● We can try to overcome the weaknesses.

● We can concentrate on the strengths.

It's impossible to take both approaches at the same time. So we should select the one that's most effective: Concentrate on the child's strengths. **When we're trying to build responsibility, it works better to work from where the child is, rather than from where we wish he was.** Then, as he gets stronger and stronger in that area, he'll be more and more able to build up his weaknesses on his own.

Which makes more sense—to work with a child from where we wish he was or to work from where he actually is?

15

Every child has the basic ingredients it takes to make a responsible person. The parent's key is to work from those ingredients, not to continually try to introduce new ones into the batch.

Rearing a child is like taking a trip. The child's abilities are the vehicle you're both riding in, and the destination is *responsibility*. What's the quickest and surest way to take the trip—to ride along on the child's strong abilities, or to try to bolster the weak abilities and then ride on them? The answer is obvious. You don't go from New York to Los Angeles in a car you've just repaired. You take the one that's never broken down—and you know never will.

How We View the World

This idea of strengths and weaknesses can be illustrated by looking at just one part of our personalities—how we view the world. Each of us is dominated by one sense of perception, and that sense overpowers all the others.

Listen to what people say when they talk to you, and you'll know what their dominant sense is:

"I *see* what you mean." (visually dominant)

"Thanks for making it *clear* to me." (visually dominant)

"That *rings* a bell." (hearing dominant)

"Why won't you *hear* me out?" (hearing dominant)

"Keep in *touch*, okay?" (touch dominant)

"That idea *feels* good to me." (touch dominant)

A person's dominant sense, at least in communication, is one of his strengths. You can try to change it to something else—or you can work with that strength to accomplish what you want to do.

> "My daughter Marcy uses her whole body in communication. When she wants to tell me something, she dances all over the room while she talks.
>
> "For a while it drove me and Andrea nuts. 'Hold still while you talk to me!' I'd say. 'I can't stand it the way you dance all over the place.' So Marcy would hold still—and would instantly become tongue-tied. When she could dance again, she'd be able to talk.

Marcy found it hard to talk without using a lot of body language. By working with her from that point, her parents were able to be more effective in teaching responsibility.

"I guess in one way, Marcy's means of expression is a strength: someday she may become a great dancer. Even if she doesn't, she's able to experience a perception of the world most of us don't even know about.

"But in another way, that strength is a weakness: she drives some people crazy when she talks to them. And she may have some hard times when she gets to school and can't dance when she answers the teacher!

"I learned that for now, though, the way to teach Marcy responsibility is to build on her strength. I've decided I need to let her communicate in the way she knows best. And communicate back with her in the same way.

"At first I'd say, 'Marcy, go clean your room.' She hardly even heard me. Then I learned the trick. Now I get up off my chair and dance in front of her. 'Marcy,' I say as I dance, 'go clean your room.'

" 'Okay,' she dances back, and off she goes to clean her room!"

What's a Parent to Do?

Every child has the makings of a responsible person. It's easy to get distracted by weaknesses. But instead, we can watch for strengths:

- The child shows special love to your new baby.
- The child is a good friend.
- The child likes to help in the kitchen.
- The child is consistently truthful, even when he or she knows punishment may result.
- The child likes to read.
- The child likes to talk.
- The child is a good listener.
- The child is observant.
- The child cares about the feelings of others.
- The child has a desire to please you.

The key is to find a point of strength, and then work from there. Strengths are the source of results when it comes to responsibility.

"You Think Funny!"

Children often think differently from adults. We shouldn't really expect them to think the same. Yet we need to remember that sometimes a child may look irresponsible to us when he's being perfectly reasonable to himself.

Truck Hats

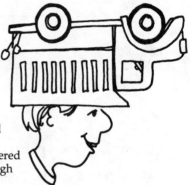

"I once asked one of my boys to pick up his toys. He scurried around and picked up a few. Then he got involved in something else.

" 'Ronnie, *pick up your toys!'* I reminded.

"He scurried around again, and got them all picked up but his dump truck. Then he wandered around the room acting as though his job was all done.

"I knew he could see the dump truck. 'Hey,' I yelled. 'Get with it!'

"He acted like he didn't even hear me.

" 'Your toys!' I shouted. 'Pick up your stupid toys before I throw them in the trash!'

"He looked at me like I had wandered in from some other planet. 'What's with this kid?' I muttered to myself. Then I realized that for him the dump truck was not a toy, it was a hat. He often wore it around like a hat. 'Hey, Ronnie,' I said. 'Now pick up your hat!' He immediately walked over to the truck, plopped it on his head, and took it out of the room."

Ronnie wasn't being irresponsible. He was just looking at things in a different way from how his mother did.

Everyone has a different viewpoint, depending on their age, sex, social level, background, and so forth. That viewpoint invariably affects their perception of responsibility.

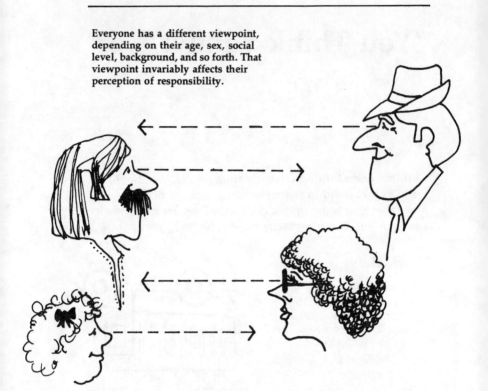

Changing Viewpoints

And kids look at things differently at different ages. Here's the advancement of Alan through his developing years;

- **1st grade:** best reader of all the boys in his class—but he doesn't like it because he's the only boy in the top reading group

- **5th grade:** does poorly in school, on purpose, so the "cool" guys will like him

- **7th grade:** wishes he read better so he could be in a reading group with the cute, smart girls—but doesn't admit it to his friends

- **8th grade:** finally admits he likes girls

- **12th grade:** no time for sports because of girls

Priorities change as we go through life, and it's our priorities that determine what things we're responsible about. We look at our kids and complain because they won't stop playing to brush their teeth. "They're irresponsible," we say.

Yet how often will we go do something that needs to be done when we're in the middle of reading the paper, or when we're engrossed in a TV show? It's not that we're irresponsible, we hasten to explain—it's just a matter of priorities!

And with kids it's often the same.

What's a Parent to Do?

We should never forget that kids see things differently from the way we do. They think differently. And that will color all that they do and say. The result: our actions may seem irresponsible to them (if they have that concept yet), and their actions will seem irresponsible to us.

Whenever we're having a problem with one of our children, we should put ourselves into his shoes. Why is he acting the way he is? What's the real problem? What's going on in his head? What's he thinking? What's he feeling? Only when we have the answers to these questions will we really be able to understand our children—and then to motivate them to be responsible.

What's the best way to find out what a child thinks and feels? One word: **LISTEN!**

Here's an example of how a misunderstanding can lead to trouble—and to more misunderstanding:

Father to child: "What do you want for breakfast?"

Child to Father: "Just give me some of those damn Cheerios." Shocked father spanks the child and sends him crying to his room.

Father to next child: "Well, what do *you* want for breakfast?"

Second Child: "I'm not sure, but I do know I don't want any of those damn Cheerios!"

The Secret of Unconditional Love

Picture an old house. The first step on the outside stairs is broken, which makes it darn hard to even get into the house.

Before the house can really become usable, that first step has to be fixed.

The same thing is true with responsibility. If the house represents responsible actions, the child has to get past the first step before he can get into the house. The first step: *Love*.

Before a parent can get a child to act responsibly, the parent must first show the child love. **When a child believes his parents truly love him, he is usually more responsive to their teachings.**

The Right Kind of Love

The best kind of love to show a child is *unconditional love*. What is unconditional love? It's the kind that says:

- I love you when you behave.

- I love you when you misbehave.

- I love you when you're polite.

- I love you when you're rude.

- I love you when you're quiet.

- I love you when you scream at your sister.

- I love you when you do your chores.

- I love you when you're totally irresponsible.

When a parent loves unconditionally, he separates the *person* of the child from the child's actions. That doesn't mean he doesn't seek to help the child improve. But he loves the child both when the child does well and when he doesn't.

- It's difficult to care about others if you don't feel others care about you.

- The child who feels cared for begins to sense that each human being is precious and different.

- Knowing that someone else cares about you is the first step to becoming responsible.

"No amount of water can drown a fish, and no amount of real love can smother a child."

Richard Moore

What's a Parent to Do?

The first step is to tell the child you love him. And do it often.

The second step is to show the love, which may be more difficult. It's not always easy to *show* a child you love him—especially when he's doing nothing right and everything wrong. When he's lying asleep in his bed, his face peaceful and angelic, it's hard to picture how you could ever have yelled at him earlier in the day. But when he gets up in the morning, his bed wet and his pajamas soaking, your reasons come back all too vividly.

Yet a mother or father can train herself or himself to love unconditionally. "Let's find a solution to this problem. I want to help you because I love you." Loving unconditionally is a state of mind, a philosophy, a way of looking at the world. It takes practice, and setbacks come easily.

But the very effort is beneficial. It helps the parent to become more the kind of person she or he wants to be. And, in the process, it builds the child too. Probably nothing else brings as many benefits for the effort expended.

The best kind of love is unconditional—the parent gives it no matter what!

A No-Fail Way to Make a Child Irresponsible

Once upon a time there was a young lady named Cinderella. She had a wicked stepmother and two wicked stepsisters—and, boy, did they ever keep Cinderella hopping! She had to—

- do the laundry
- wash the dishes
- scrub the floor
- fix the mending
- chop the wood
- start the fire
- cook the meals
- plant the seeds in the garden
- water the garden
- weed the garden
- harvest the garden

And that was only the beginning! No wonder she needed magic to make her look nice after all that! You'd have to look hard to find a dirtier or grubbier person than Cinderella. She didn't even take time to wash up after cleaning out the fireplace—she just went straight in and made supper!

Cinderella's problem wasn't that she wasn't responsible. Instead, she just didn't have the time or energy to fix herself up. We all have a limited amount of energy to use each day. If we use a lot doing one thing, we won't have as much left over for the next task. There's a simple name for this common problem. It's called the Cinderella Factor.

Here's what the Cinderella Factor means in terms of responsibility: **If a child is given more than he can handle, he'll invariably end up being irresponsible.** If we want irresponsible children, the approach is easy enough: just give them too much to do. But if we want responsibility, well . . .

> "When Richard Sr. and I decided to go out for the evening, we asked Richard Jr. to babysit the younger kids. He was willing enough. But when we got home, we couldn't believe the mess that was waiting for us. Dishes were piled high in the sink. Clothes were strewn all over the house. Dog footprints were on the carpet and kitchen linoleum. And the baby had been put to bed without a change of diaper.
>
> "I was furious! Then I saw something that made me maddest of all: Richard Jr. was in the family room asleep in front of the TV. That was the last straw.
>
> " 'Wake up, you lazy lout,' I shouted at him. I was standing right over him, and he didn't even stir. 'Come on!' I yelled. 'Wake up and help with this mess. I can't believe you'd be so irresponsible!' But his eyelids didn't even flicker.
>
> "Then I started to think. He'd been snow skiing all day before he came home to babysit. He'd left at six in the morning, and that was after a late evening the night before. The truth flashed in my head like a bomb. Richard Jr. wasn't being irresponsible. He was just plain exhausted!"

Energy Drain

If you hook up a battery to operate a light, it will give you a nice bright shine. But what if you hook up the battery to operate a light, a radio, a toaster, a refrigerator, and a space

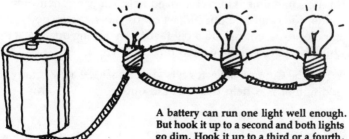

A battery can run one light well enough. But hook it up to a second and both lights go dim. Hook it up to a third or a fourth, and pretty soon you don't have any light. You don't have anything left in the battery either.

heater? If the light shines at all, it will be pretty feeble. The battery just doesn't have enough energy to run all that stuff.

And a human being, children included, is just the same. We all have a finite amount of energy. If we use it up, it's gone—and we won't be able to do much after that.

"Marty used to get good grades, "One mother says. "Now he's really slipping. He's becoming such an irresponsible kid!"

On the surface Marty's mother is right. But she hasn't looked deeply enough. Marty hasn't become irresponsible. Instead, he's simply running out of energy. In addition to his schoolwork, he now has student council, debate squad, basketball team, and a part-time job. No wonder he doesn't have enough energy to get good grades as well!

When a child fails to be responsible, it doesn't necessarily mean he just isn't a responsible-type person. Instead he may simply be spread too thin. Too many things hooked up to one battery make the light go dim.

What's a Parent to Do?

If a normally responsible child starts to be irresponsible, the problem might be that he's suffering from the dreaded energy drain. Take a look at his life. Is he doing more than he used to be doing? Is he trying to do too much? Does he seem tired? Does he seem crabby (more than usual)?

When a person gets overloaded, he doesn't need motivation to be more responsible. He needs someone to help him lighten his load.

At the same time, kids often need help knowing their own limits. Kids can be poor judges of just how much they can handle. A parent can do a big favor by pointing out when a child is trying to take on too much.

When the Cinderella Factor hits your house, be a good fairy godmother and help the poor kid out!

If You Rely on This, You're Headed for Trouble!

"Shape up!"
"No, you shape up!"
"No, YOU shape up!"

"Hey, get on the stick! Shape up! You start being a better parent, and I mean right now! After all, you really ought to be a better parent, you know!"

There. It's done! Now that you've read that line, you're a better parent, aren't you—whether you needed it or not.

What made this magical transformation? An exhortation!—the wonderful and powerful tool of getting someone to change just by telling them they ought to.

There's only one problem. That wonderful and powerful tool doesn't work worth beans. **Exhortation is the method most commonly used to increase responsibility. It's also the least effective.**

Mom and dad decided to take Mark and Kevin out to a restaurant. The last time the boys had been noisy and messy, but mom and dad were in the mood to go out to eat, so they thought they'd give it a try.

"Boys," dad said, "you be sure to be quiet while we go to the restaurant."

They went in and they ordered. The food hadn't even come before Mark started to make noise with his silverware. Kevin soon joined in.

"Boys," dad said, "you need to be quiet."

They didn't respond.

"Mark! Kevin! If you're not quiet you're going to be sorry!"

Mom spoke up. "Boys, when we're in restaurants we need to be quiet so we don't bother the other customers."

You can imagine their response. Mark and Kevin didn't really care about the other customers. What they cared about was that they were having fun.

Exhortation doesn't do much good at all in getting people to be responsible. That's as true for kids as for anybody.

Look back to the start of this section and review the exhortation there, the one to be a better parent. It didn't work, did it? In fact, it probably was counterproductive—if anything, it made you feel resentful and rebellious.

Consider how effective these exhortations are:

- Politician to voter: "You really ought to get out and vote, you know. Voting is important."

- Teacher to student: "You really ought to learn how to read better, you know."

- Boss to worker: "You really ought to work harder, you know."

- Kid to cat:"You really shouldn't poop in my sandpile, you know."

And then consider if these parent-to-child exhortations are any more effective:

- "You really ought to pick up your dirty socks, you know."

- "You really ought to do your chores, you know."

- "You really ought to stop throwing food on the floor, you know."

- "You really ought to be well-behaved, you know."

What's a Parent to Do?

What's a parent to do? Whenever you're tempted to exhort your child into being responsible, DON'T! (How's that for an exhortation!) When we use exhortation, we're taking away the child's self-motivation. And when someone loses self-motivation, they either ignore the request or they resent it—or both.

Much better is to help the child be motivated by giving:

rewards
praise
choices
the child something he values

- **Instead of** "You really ought to pick up your dirty socks, you know," **try this:** "As soon as your socks are picked up I'll read you a story."

- **Instead of** "You really ought to make your bed, you know," **try this:** "You sure did a great job of making your bed yesterday. It made your whole room look nicer!

- **Instead of** "You really ought to do your chores, you know," **try this:** "Would you rather do your chores just before breakfast or right after?"

- **Instead of** "You really ought to stop throwing food on the floor, you know," **try this:** "Eat neatly for just a week and then we'll all go out to a restaurant for two nights in a row!"

- **Instead of** "You really ought to be well-behaved, you know," **try this:** "I like the way you were quiet when I was talking on the phone to Aunt Betty."

There's No Excuse for This

"Excuses are like armpits: everybody has them and they all smell."

Author unknown

We don't have to look far to find good excuses (as well as poor ones). If we aren't masters of rationalization, the guy next door sure is!

- The golfer misses an easy shot. "This blamed golf club!" he exclaims.

- The lady walks down the street—and stumbles. Instantly she looks back to see what caused her tripping. She's much too graceful to stumble by herself.

- The student gets a poor grade: "The teacher doesn't like me," he complains.

- The worker fails to get a promotion. "I got screwed up by office politics," he says. "The boss gave the job to his nephew."

None of these people looked to the real source of the problem—themselves. The reason so many people get so good at making excuses is that they had so much practice when they were kids.

But there's a problem. **Excuse making is the antithesis of accepting responsibility.** If the man blames the golf club, instead of himself, he's saying the fault was outside himself. He doesn't accept the real reason for his failure. He shys away from the responsibility.

An important part of learning to be responsible is discovering what shapes our behavior. It isn't events or circumstances or other people. It's ourselves.

When a child is allowed to escape responsibility for his actions, when his parents let him make excuses, they're teaching him to be *ir*responsible. He's learning that he can explain away the misbehavior, that he can place blame elsewhere—and get away from it.

> "In our home, we've learned that we shouldn't accept excuses for being late at the supper table. That only disrupts the family. After some trial and error, we established this system:
>
> "Supper is served at 6 o'clock sharp. If you come a little late, you can still eat—if there's any left for you. You have to eat the food cold unless you're big enough to heat it up for yourself. Then you can reheat the meal—if there's any left!
>
> "Each week I buy exactly what food we'll need for that week. My menus are planned very tightly, so the latecomer can't raid the refrigerator.
>
> "Having that simple approach has made a lot of difference. Before, it seemed like I was fixing four meals every night. But now that I have the rule of no excuses, I only fix one every night. And everyone is there to eat it!"

Insurance Excuses

Metropolitan Life Insurance Company once reported the following excuses people give for their automobile accidents. Somewhere the people giving these excuses were taught that they could get away with irresponsibility through placing blame elsewhere.

- "An invisible car came out of nowhere, struck my car, and vanished."

- "The other car collided with mine without warning me of its intention."

- "I had been driving my car for 40 years when I fell asleep at the wheel and had the accident."

- "As I reached an intersection, a hedge sprang up, obscuring my vision."

- "I pulled away from the side of the road, glanced at my mother-in-law, and headed over the embankment."

- "The pedestrian had no idea which direction to go, so I ran over him."

- "The telephone pole was approaching fast. I attempted to swerve out of its path when it struck my front end."

- "The guy was all over the road. I had to swerve a number of times before I hit him."

What's a Parent to Do?

Excuses are destructive. The more a child learns to make excuses, the less he'll learn to be responsible. There's no excuse for excuses!

To teach a child *not* to make excuses, take these simple steps:

1. Don't *invite* the child to make excuses by asking why he failed to do the responsible thing.

2. Don't make excuses for the child.

3. Never accept an excuse or alibi offered by the child.

4. Help the child learn the difference between making excuses and accepting responsibility.

5. Reward children for their responsible behavior, not their alibis. If possible, give a reward that's naturally or logically tied to the behavior.

6. Try to be as flexible as possible in setting and enforcing family rules.

7. Avoid making excuses yourself!

Give 'Em What They Deserve!

Betty bought a red wagon for her seven children. They were pretty excited. Almost as if it had been rehearsed, all seven raced for the wagon and tried to climb on. It's pretty hard to fit seven kids on one wagon—as they quickly discovered. But the kids pushed and pulled and tugged and squeezed until finally all seven were loaded on.

They sat there for a minute, waiting expectantly for someone to pull them. But there wasn't anyone to pull—all the potential pullers were loaded on the wagon.

It was a great lesson in natural consequences. If no one helps do the work that's involved in helping others have fun, *no one will have fun.*

That's when they started to cooperate. One of the older ones got off the wagon and started to pull. Then another took his turn. The next couple of hours the kids had a great time—and all from a lesson they'd learned totally on their own.

The Consequences of Life

Many parents just love to step in and help their children work things out. And they like to impose punishments from outside the situation.

"If I don't get involved, how in the world is my child ever going to learn?" I know the concern; I've had it myself.

But there's a better way. It's to *let the situation itself determine the consequences of the child's acts.* There's really no better way to help a child learn the importance of being responsible.

The approach: the use of natural and logical consequences.

Natural consequences: Where the child has to experience the consequences that will naturally flow from his acts if no one else interferes. If he throws his food on the floor, he doesn't have any food anymore, and he goes hungry. (If the child is big enough to get into the refrigerator between meals, the natural consequences won't follow, and the parent will need to impose logical consequences for throwing food.)

Logical consequences: Where the parent intervenes to impose consequences that are logically connected to the child's behavior. These are generally used when there are no natural consequences (the child hits his little brother—the only natural consequence is the brother gets hurt; but the logical consequence is that the child gets removed from the brother and sent to his room) or where the natural consequence is harmful (the child runs in front of a car—the natural consequence is that he gets hit; instead the parent rescues the child and imposes the logical consequence that the child doesn't get to play outside anymore).

The more a child experiences the results of his own actions, the more likely he'll learn to be responsible for what he does. The parent who consistently creates artificial consequences (like spanking and yelling) will end up with a child (and later an adult) who is irresponsible. The child will see no connection between his behavior and the results of the behavior.

In the same way, the parent who consistently shelters his child from the results of his acts is creating a person who doesn't recognize a responsibility for those acts. The child never learns that some acts can be harmful both to others and to himself.

If a child plays with fire, the natural consequence is that he may get burned. A parent can't allow that, so logical consequences must be used instead: the child has to stay indoors for the next two days.

Getting to School on Time

Stella had a child, Joey, who just couldn't get to school on time. It was a problem in three ways:

1. It was a real hassle for Stella and her husband, Ray, to try to get him there on time. It messed up their morning.

2. It made Joey miss some of his schooling every day.

3. It disrupted the class when Joey arrived.

Stella and Ray struggled with the problem until they decided to play it smart and use logical consequences. They talked to the teacher and got her to agree to hold Joey after school on the days he was late. He *hated* being held late. All the other kids were running off having a good time and he had to just sit there having no fun at all.

Stella stopped nagging him to get to school. In fact, she didn't say much at all. If he was on time, great—he didn't have to stay late. But if he arrived late, he did have to stay afterwards.

It didn't take long. Only two or three times staying late and suddenly Joey started getting to school on time every day.

Natural and logical consequences work like magic when it comes to teaching kids to be responsible for their own acts!

What's a Parent to Do?

Life, all by itself, will do a great job of teaching our children certain aspects of responsibility. All we have to do is let nature take its course! Sometimes we can't let the natural consequences happen to our child, though, and in those instances we can apply the idea of logical consequences.

Natural and logical consequences will help the child see that the unpleasant things that happen to him are a result of his own actions—and the same will apply to the pleasant!

Want a carefree, foolproof method of parenting? This is it. Just about all a parent has to do is let it happen!

A Surefire Way of Getting Children Interested

Angela preferred to take care of her family's meals all by herself. She had a daughter, Sara, aged nine, who could help, but it was more trouble to supervise Sara than it was to do the job herself.

But one day Angela decided to let Sara get involved. She put aside a good portion of one day for the meal. She let Sara decide what to make, based on the ingredients they had in the house. Sara prepared the ingredients, cooked the meal, and served it. Mom assumed the secondary role of helper.

The result was surprising to both: Sara did an excellent job. And she really enjoyed it. The job was quite a challenge—and that's what made it best of all.

Children who are allowed to stretch toward their potential tend to develop more responsibility.

Children we never expect much from become adults who don't do much. The reason is that they never learned how to meet challenges.

All people need a chance to be challenged in life, to stretch to new things. Children are no exception. They need to be given as much responsibility as they can handle to help them to progress.

What's a Parent to Do?

Meeting challenges is exciting for anyone, and children are no exception. You, as a parent, can encourage your children to meet challenges by—

Helping the child see that challenges are fun.

Puzzles and riddles are enjoyable for one reason—they force the person to stretch a little. Give your child puzzles and other educational games. These will help you to help your child to grow.

Giving your child the joy of knowing he or she is growing and developing.

It's a thrill to learn new things, to be able to do new things. If you're not moving forward, you're probably moving backward. And that's a bad feeling for anyone. Constantly expose your child to new ideas, to new skills, and his motion will ever be forward!

Children can become frustrated and discouraged if they aren't being challenged. But give them a chance to stretch and they'll feel better about themselves.

Praising the growth you see in your child.

A little praise and recognition go a long way toward building a child. When children feel that others see them as people capable of meeting challenges, they'll be responsive to new situations.

By following these principles, one mother raised some exceptional children:

- one daughter is a champion ballet skier
- one son is a basketball starter at a major university
- one daughter is an opera singer
- one son is a highly successful lawyer

In an interview, this mother explained her approach. It all added up to helping her children meet new challenges throughout their lives. She stressed that a parent should:

- always be supportive
- always stress the positive
- put each child in the setting of challenges
- provide opportunities for each to grow
- refuse to be possessive—let the child excel in the area *he's* interested in
- help the child to stretch by being patiently supportive. Let the child grow into his own unique abilities.

Try This and You'll Be Amazed at the Results

"Randy, will you please go out and pick the peaches?" dad asked.

"Sure, dad," Randy said. He'd never picked peaches before, but it couldn't be that hard! He went out to the peach trees in their backyard and took a good look. The branches were kind of high. He went to get the ladder. But it was kind of heavy.

Randy thought about his problem. Then he had an idea! He went up to the tree and began to shake it. Shake, shake! The peaches started to fall to the ground. *I'll bet dad never thought of this great way of picking peaches!* Randy thought.

After a few minutes dad came to the back door. "How are you doing out there, Randy?" dad yelled.

"Just fine!" Randy shouted back.

"Okay!" Dad went back into the house.

An hour later Randy went into the house to show dad his work. "I'm all done," he said proudly. "I found I great new way of picking them."

When they arrived at the tree, dad looked down at the ground. Peach mush! His face got red and his lips began to quiver in anger. . . .

Randy thought he was doing a good job. But he didn't have any good instruction to start with, and he didn't have any feedback as he went.

It's hard for people to know how they're doing unless they have some means of measuring their progress. As children grow in responsibility, their parents need to help them know *how much* they're growing.

The key is good communication. **The more feedback a child gets on how he's doing, the more likely it is that he'll be responsible.** The communication should tell the child:

- how he's doing, • where he stands, • that he's loved.

Benny was playing with blocks in his room. His mom walked by, then came back and poked her head in. "Hey, Benny," she said, "I sure do love you!"

Melanie was helping set the table. Mom handed her some more plates to put on "I sure appreciate your help, Melanie," she said.

Dad was reading the evening newspaper when Todd swooped by wearing a towel for a cape. "Hey, Superman," dad called. "Nice to have you around." Todd grinned and swooped away.

Too often parents are all talk and no listen!

We Only Offer Twelve Seconds

A disturbing study has shown that the average parent spends only twelve seconds of *quality* time with his child every day. If the study is really accurate, it's amazing that we have as many kids turn out as well as we do. Good communication is essential to a good relationship between

40

parent and child. A good relationship is essential to having a child feel good about himself. And a child must feel good about himself before he can really develop into a responsible person.

Sometimes it's hard to say exactly what we mean when we're communicating with another person. When that's the case, we need to keep trying, keep restating it until the child knows exactly how we feel.

Sometimes it's hard to sit down and really share feelings with another person. When we're rusty at it, we hesitate. We're a little embarrassed to open up, even to a child. When that's the case, we need to keep trying, until we're able to do it genuinely and sincerely.

What's a Parent to Do?

How often should we have meaningful communication with our children? **Every day.** A child needs to have mileposts to know how he's doing. Parents can provide those mileposts by showing the child specifically how he's doing—in love. The parent can discuss negative concerns as well as offer positive praise—but the love must always be there. It's got to be the dominant element in the relationship, as well as in the communication.

Here are some tips to help you in communicating:

- Realize there's a different language for communicating logic and communicating feelings. Children haven't learned the language of logic yet—but that's what their parents usually speak! To communicate effectively with a child, speak the language of emotion. Talk about what you *feel*.

- Send I-messages, rather than you-messages. In other words, speak from your own point of view and your own person, rather than theirs. Say "I feel upset when you don't make your bed," not "You were irresponsible because you didn't make your bed." By dealing with how you feel (through I-messages), you place the issue where it belongs: not on what happened (you-messages) but on how you feel about what happened.

- Don't prescribe remedies before you diagnose the problem. Really *listen* to what the child is saying before you try to respond. In fact, listening is probably the most important part of the communication.

- When you're talking over a problem, repeat back what the child said, to make sure you're understanding the message the same way he's sending it.

- Don't overlook the power of touch in communication. Sometimes a loving touch on the arm or shoulder, or snuggling a child on your lap, will say much more than words can ever say.

A Vital Technique That's Often Overlooked

Sometimes we talk about being responsible as if it involves making a choice between good and bad. The child will be responsible and polite, or he'll be irresponsible and impolite. The child will be responsible and obedient, or irresponsible and disobedient. He'll keep his room clean, or he won't.

All of that is true. Or at least half true. But responsibility stretches broader than that. Responsibility also involves sacrifice—giving up something good for something better. **As a child learns how to sacrifice, he'll also be learning how to be more responsible.**

Suppose, for example, that a child wants to have a pet. To be able to care for the pet, the child must be responsible. He must be willing to sacrifice for the pet.

To help your child understand the idea of sacrifice, relate it to something he can understand. Help him see that everything has a price tag.

The thing that gets sacrificed isn't necessarily bad. Maybe the child has been spending fifteen minutes a day reading that he won't be able to spend now. Or maybe he's been playing with friends that extra few minutes. But now he needs to spend the time with his pet.

Another example: Lisa likes to play the piano. She's been taking piano lessons for three years now, and she's quite good. She's moved from "Mary Had a Little Lamb" to some light classical works.

But now her grades are slipping in school and her mom and dad feel she's spending too much time with the piano. She gets home from school and either plays with friends, or talks on the phone, or plays the piano. It's nice that she wants to be good on the piano, and that she enjoys it. But she's not being responsible when it comes to her schoolwork.

The answer: she needs to sacrifice. She doesn't have to give the piano up entirely, but she does need to get more balanced in her approach. She needs to spend some time on schoolwork *as well as* the piano.

By sacrificing the good for the better, a child becomes more and more responsible. Every bit of success we experience has a price—and the price we sometimes have to pay for responsibility is *sacrifice*.

Always a Trade-off

Children have limits. Whenever we ask them to do something new, chances are that they'll have to give up something they've been doing in the past.

There's nothing wrong with that. But we need to recognize what's happening. If we're asking our children to sacrifice, we need to know that's what we're doing.

For example, if a mother asks her son to come home from his friend's house a few minutes early to help set the table, she's asking him to sacrifice some of his playing time.

If a father asks a daughter to help him in the yard for an hour every Saturday, he's cutting into some of her precious free time.

If the mother asks the daughter to make her bed, she's

asking the daughter to sacrifice some of her laziness (which sometimes is a very real commodity!)

If the father asks the son to brush his teeth, the boy has to sacrifice a few minutes he's spent reading each morning.

Then the father and mother wonders why their kids won't respond. It's such a reasonable request!

The reason, of course, isn't that the child doesn't want to be responsible. Instead, the problem is that the child doesn't want to make the sacrifice.

What's a Parent to Do?

There are two things a parent can do to help their children accept the sacrifices they must make. The first is simply to understand the reasons for the child's hesitations or disobedience, to understand the idea of sacrifice and trade-offs, and to help the child understand it too.

The second thing a parent can do is to give the child a payoff. It's hard to motivate someone to do something unless there's something in it for him:

"I know you'd rather play than help me in the yard. But if you can spend an hour and help me, I'll be able to spend some time with you later in the day."

"I know you'd rather read than brush your teeth. But if you carefully brush your teeth, you'll have fewer cavities. And I'll let you stay up an extra five minutes every night."

"I know you'd rather stay at your friend's house than help set the table. But if you can help me that way, I'll have the time to read you a story just before you go to bed."

I'm *not* describing a form of bribery here. Human nature is constructed in such a way that before a person will make a sacrifice, he must anticipate a payoff. In helping our children receive payoffs, we must be careful that we *don't* give bribes (candy, money, and the like) and instead give a benefit that's naturally tied to the responsibility.

To get responsibility ya gotta give up something else. We'll be more successful in helping our children give—and get—if we make it all worthwhile for them.

"I'm Running Out of Patience!"

Three-year-old Rex kept spilling his food at dinner time. For a while his parents cleaned up after him, but then they reached the point where they felt he was ready to accept responsibility for his messy acts. The next time Rex spilled they had him get down on the floor and pick the food up—every bit of it. He spilled again at the next meal, and they had him pick it up.

It wasn't long before he was cured of that particular bad habit.

A neighbor had a two-year-old daughter, June, who had the same problem. June just loved to throw her food on the floor. When the neighbor heard of her friend's success with Rex, she decided to try the approach with June. When June spilled peas, the mother had her get down to clean them up. June picked up a few and then wandered off. The mother put her back to finish. Before long June was rolling on the floor—right in the peas. She never did get them picked up. And the approach never worked.

What was the neighbor doing wrong? Absolutely nothing. The only problem was that June was younger than Rex, and therefore had a lower patience level.

It's important to recognize that different kids have different patience levels. The attention span of a two-year-old is different from that of a three-year-old. A ten-year-old has a different patience level than an adult does. **The higher a child's patience level, the better he'll be able to handle responsibility.**

Kids Are Different

Often we treat kids as though they had the same patience level as we do. And then when it doesn't work we wonder why they're so naughty. They're not naughty, of course; they're just not as mature.

Even adults are limited in their patience level. Research has shown that adults have a limited patience level when they're watching information films. The longest that kind of film can run is twelve minutes. Longer than that and it starts to lose the audience. Shorter than that and it holds the audience even better.

Everyone has a different patience level, depending on his or her maturity—and how things are going that day!

Grandpa likes to play with jigsaw puzzles. He can keep it up for hours.

Sis has a high patience level when it comes to talking. But not listening!

Dad isn't so patient with jigsaw puzzles. "They drive me nuts!" he says.

Little brother has a low attention span for just about everything.

Mom loves to read. But she gets impatient at soap operas.

A five-year-old has an attention span of only a few minutes. If his parents want to take the child to something that lasts longer, they'll have problems—unless the activity reengages the child's attention periodically, like a cartoon movie usually will.

Ask any parent who takes a young child to church. They'll verify that the child's patience level is very well defined. And it's quite short. The answer: either avoid taking the child to church, or give the child something else to do while he's there. If the parent doesn't take one of those choices, he's going to end up with a crabby child at church!

Of course, as the child grows older, her patience level will rise. Eventually she'll learn to listen to the sermon and be quiet in church.

What's a Parent to Do?

The child's patience level will determine how soon he's ready for additional responsibility. If parents try to thrust it on the child too soon, the result will be failure and frustration. Parents should give new responsibility only when the patience level has reached the point where the child can handle it.

If a child is pushed too fast, he won't be able to respond. His level is too low. Before you give any new responsibility to your child, try to figure out if he's ready for it. If you think he is, but find out later that he's not, don't be afraid to withdraw it. You can try again later.

The same applies to expecting certain kinds of behaviors from your child. A three-year-old will sometimes act as mature as a six-year-old—but not for as long. His patience level won't sustain it.

Match yourself to your child's level, and he'll be able to grow at his own pace.

But MY Kid Never Keeps the Rules!

A religious leader was once complimented on the spiritual strength of his people. "How do you do it?" he was asked.

"It's not as hard as you might imagine," he responded. "I teach them correct principles and let them govern themselves."

That approach, which has proven to work over and over again, is a good one for parents to follow: **Teach children correct principles and then let them rule themselves.** Not only does the approach help children learn responsibility, but it helps them to use it for the right reasons.

Teach Principles, Not Just Rules

Every child needs to know family rules. Rules are what make a family function well. But there's something even more important: children should be taught the *reason* for the rules. They need to know the principle that caused the rule to be formed in the first place.

Rule:

Don't talk with your mouth full.

Principle:

Be polite to others—don't show them a mouth full of food. And they may not be able to understand your speech when your tongue is busy with food.

Rule:

Don't fight and argue.

Principle:

You and those around you will be happier if you are loving and kind to other people.

Rule:

Don't try to get more than your share.

Principle:

You will feel happier if you make sure that everyone gets a fair portion.

What's a Parent to Do?

Obedience to rules is important. That's one useful way of measuring how responsible a child is. But the inner character of the child is even more important. Old-time moral *principles* need to be taught along with rules.

The child who is obedient, who doesn't fight with his brothers and sisters, and who cleans his room, does his chores, and gets good grades will, by all appearances, be a model of responsibility. But none of that will mean a thing, once he gets away from the parental eye, if he hasn't made the underlying principles a part of his character. True responsibility is the ability to respond correctly to a given situation. Correct principles are necessary before a person can make that response.

Doing chores is important—but let the child know the underlying principle: It makes you feel good to know that you're doing your share.

Cleaning up the bedroom is important—but don't forget the underlying principle: Neatness is important to a feeling of well-being.

Getting along with others is important—but keep in mind the virtues that make it possible: forgiveness, tolerance, love.

An Unavoidable Part of Teaching Responsibility

"When I was ten I decided I wanted to get a newspaper route. My mom and dad were willing to let me. But there was one catch: I had to go out every day, through rain and snow and sleet and heat.

"One winter day I got up and looked out the window and saw three feet of snow. *Maybe I won't go out today,* I thought to myself. *The subscribers will understand.*

"But my parents wouldn't hear about it. 'You agreed to take this route,' mom said. 'And now you're going to do what you agreed.'

"I thought she was being pretty unrealistic. But she helped me bundle up against the cold and then helped me load up my sled. I trudged out through the snow, delivering those stupid papers, complaining at my mom the whole way. 'Why couldn't she take me in the car?' I muttered to myself. 'Why couldn't we just skip the whole thing today?'

"I didn't stop to think that a car couldn't even travel in that kind of snow. And I wouldn't have cared if it could. All I cared about is that I didn't want to deliver those papers!"

Teaching responsibility can be a risky thing. The mom in that story faced some real risks in requiring her boy to be responsible. He might have caught a cold or pneumonia. She might have alienated him. **But risk is an unavoidable part of teaching responsibility.** It's virtually impossible to try to get one without having the other.

If there is no risk, there is no chance for failure. Where there is no chance for failure, there is little chance for real success. And where there is little chance for success, there is little chance that responsibility can be developed.

"When I was in high school my parents gave me a key to the house. 'We trust you,' they said. 'You're nearly an adult now, and we feel you're mature enough to use this key wisely.'

"In giving me the key they faced some real risks. I could have abused my privilege and stayed out all night. I could have used the key to bring girls into the house when my parents were out of town.

51

"But they were willing to face the risk in return for teaching me something about responsibility. At the same time, they set up the risk in such a way that they could control it. I always knew they'd be there with one eye on me, watching how I was doing!"

My Super-Protective Neighbor

Mrs. Wilson was super protective of her little girl, Amy. Amy didn't get to leave the yard without an escort. She wasn't allowed to walk to school with her friends—her mom or dad had to drive her. She never got to stay overnight, like everyone else did—her mom was afraid to have her gone after dark.

For a while everything seemed to go okay. Amy seemed happy at school and had a good time with her friends. But then, gradually, things began to change. Amy didn't mature as fast as her friends. She wasn't allowed to go do things with them, and she didn't have enough experiences to progress as fast as they were.

Amy is now an adult—but she's still below average in development. She started out on a level with everyone else, but her home circumstances just wouldn't let her keep up.

It could be that Mrs. Wilson ruined her daughter for life. All because she was trying to protect Amy from the big, bad world. In the process, Amy *was* safe. But she never matured into a responsible adult.

People must learn to risk if they hope to have success. Those who try to have one without the other are only fooling themselves.

What's a Parent to Do?

As we try to build responsibility in our kids, they may want to hold back sometimes. They'll recognize the risk and try to avoid it. Or *we* may want to hold back, because we won't want them to suffer the risk.

But, try as you might, you can't get away from the risk. Growth and risk are synonymous, at least in some ways.

The answer: grit your teeth and move ahead. If you can, make conditions ideal for your child. But there's a limit to what you can do. Try to overcontrol things and the child will end up with no growth at all.

Taking risks is worth it. Take reasonable risks, and you're more apt to end up with a responsible child, one who will be a strong member of society from youth to old age. Avoid risks and you'll end up with an emotional basket-case. Like Mrs. Wilson did.

Little Things That Help in Teaching Responsibility

"When I was in junior high I threw a snowball at a girl in my class. My shot was straight and true. The only problem was that a teacher walked into the snowball's path before it hit target.

"She promptly marched me to the principal's office, where I was punished. And then the worst part of all happened: they called my dad. I knew I was going to catch heck and a half.

"But dad didn't say much. He didn't yell. He told me he knew my hitting the teacher was an accident, and said I should be more careful about throwing snowballs. Then dad told me about a time when *he* was taken to the principal's office for throwing snowballs.

"The few minutes he spent with me that day were just a little thing—but they're one of the things I remember best about my junior high years."

The little things can be very effective in teaching responsibility. In fact, it's the little things added together that make the most impact.

When a child shows you something he's made, don't just grunt and go back to your newspaper. Take a good look. Then praise him for his efforts.

Have you ever been to the beach? The sand stretches out for hundreds of yards. There must be millions of grains of sand there. You walk out across it and don't even think of it. You can roll in it and enjoy every minute of it.

But what happens when you get one little grain of that sand in your eye? Suddenly the little thing means a lot!

Contrast these two stories:

> "I was assigned to clean all the weeds out of my family's very messy garden. I worked and worked, all afternoon. 'Dad's going to be really proud,' I said to myself as I struggled with that hoe against the hard ground. I just knew he'd like my work. Finally I was finished. I went in to show off my work to dad.
>
> "He came right out, a big smile on his face. He took one look at my efforts and patted me on the shoulder. 'Great job,' he said. Then he leaned down and began to pick the cut weeds out of the garden. I'd seen him put grass clippings on the garden. Weeds should help it too, I'd thought. But here dad was picking the weeds out! I guess it was just a little thing, but . . .
>
> "The next year I did a *really* good job. I pulled all the weeds. And I put them all in a plastic garbage bag, so the trash men would haul them away. I worked from about 6 a.m. till nearly noon. When I was all finished, I took dad out to the garden, so I could show him. He was in a hurry—he had to go to a meeting or something. 'Looks good, looks good,' he said, hardly even glancing at it. Then he rushed off.
>
> "After that I didn't feel much like working in the garden anymore."

Now compare that story to this one:

> "Dad asked me to spade the garden so we could plant it. I went out early in the morning, so it would be cool while I worked, but it wasn't long before the temperature was over ninety. I was really roasting out there!
>
> "After what seemed like an eternity, I was finally finished. I went into the house and got my dad and asked him to come see my work. He was dressed in his suit; he was about ready to go to an important meeting. But he came on out with me.
>
> "He whistled when he saw the job I'd done. 'Hey, you're just like a professional,' he said. 'This looks really nice. I like the way you've broken all the clods down so small. And the whole plot is so smooth and even! It's hot out here, but you just kept at it, didn't you. And now we've got the best garden plot in the neighborhood!' Then he had to hurry to his meeting.
>
> "Dad was always doing little things like that—taking time to let me know how I was doing."

The Trip—or the Treatment?

Two families take their children on big trips every summer. They go to the Grand Canyon, Yellowstone Park, Disneyland, Mexico, and a lot of other fun places.

In one of the families, the parents are patient and tolerant of their children's childishness, at least most of the time. In the other family, the parents are always on their children's backs. The children can almost do nothing right.

When the children grow up, what do they remember about their childhood? They remember the annual trips, sure—but even more important is the way they were treated on the trips, the little things:

"My mom and dad didn't seem to be very happy to have children. It didn't matter what we tried, they would only growl at us—or yell."

"My mom and dad really gave me a feeling that I was an important person. They cared about who I was and what I did with myself. It was fun to be around them, because they let me be myself."

What's a Parent to Do?

The little things will help the parent-child relationship be a good one. When that relationship is strong, the children will be more interested in doing what the parents wish. Including being more responsible.

Try these:

- spend regular time with each child

- show up for plays, recitals, games the child is playing in, and so forth

- as you put your younger children to bed, review the day with them, asking what they most enjoyed, what was their biggest problem

Spend meaningful time with each child on a regular basis.

- keep a scrapbook for each child
- give surprise treats occasionally
- give hugs and loving pats

- give praise and encouragement
- when a child gets in trouble, be understanding even if you must be firm

- recognize the child's accomplishments in front of others (do this equally for all your children, so no one feels you have favorites)

- say "please" and "thank you" to your children, just as you expect them to do with you
- when you've made a mistake, don't hesitate to own up to it; don't hesitate to say "I'm sorry"
- put up a message board at a convenient place in the home, with an envelope on the board for each family member. Have a pen and paper nearby, so members of the family can write special messages of love and appreciation to other family members, inserting them in that person's envelope. Use the board often!

How a Fence Can Help a Child to Grow

It was the first day of school, and Becky was in the first grade. "You're a big enough girl that you can walk to school with your friends," mom said. "But today I want to walk with you."

Hand in hand, mother and daughter walked to school together. On the way, mom pointed out the landmarks, so Becky would be sure to know the proper route to take. And they made a plan for that afternoon.

When school got out, Becky's whole family was there waiting, according to the plan. Becky beamed—she knew she'd get to lead them all home! She moved in front of the group and began to walk. Along the way she pointed out the landmarks to her family, so they'd know the proper way if they ever had to walk to the school again.

Becky could have been sent off to school alone. But her family made her feel much more safe and secure than if they had done that. She felt loved—and protected.

The safer a child feels, the more she'll be able to learn responsibility. She needs to know that her parents love and support her. She needs to know they will always be there when she needs them. If her life lacks these things, and the security they bring, she won't feel the safety that must precede responsibility.

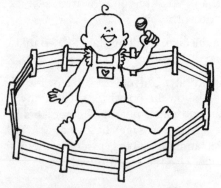

A small child needs a very small fence. He needs to feel that the parents are always close and ever-ready to help.

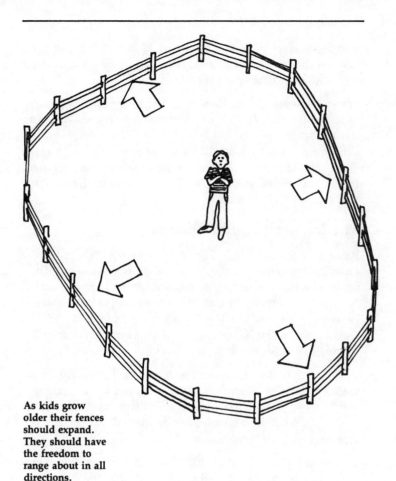

As kids grow older their fences should expand. They should have the freedom to range about in all directions.

In a safe environment, a child will feel protected against the fierce and wild world out there. She'll know that she can grow at her own pace, that she can learn independence and responsibility within her own sphere before she has to venture out.

Providing security for a child is like building a fence around her. Within the fence she's free to move and do as much as she likes. She knows that the outside world can't move in on her, as long as she stays in the fence. And she knows that you'll never leave her in the fence alone. Fences can be restricting. But they also help a child to grow!

When a person is learning to fly an airplane, he's often put in a simulator. There the experience of a flight is simulated, and the student pilot has the chance to learn while still being safe on the ground. The simulator is a fence—but it helps the student expand his skills.

When someone learns how to drive, he's not forced out onto the freeway, all alone, the first day. Instead he learns the fundamentals of handling a car while he's still in the classroom. When it's finally time to drive, the instructor is sitting in the car with him. And the instructor has his own brake, to use if necessary. It's a fence that helps the student feel safe enough to learn.

The Danger of Fence Removal

Ray was a special boy. His parents had always wanted a child, and when Ray came, he was their pride and joy. They worried about the crime rate, about the kidnapping that occurred in a nearby city, and they kept him close at hand. If he wanted to play at the neighbor's, mom or dad had to escort him over. If he wanted to sleep overnight at a friend's house, the answer was always "no."

When it came time for Ray to start school, he was afraid to walk by himself. His mom thought maybe it was time for him to move out on his own more. But she didn't assert her feelings, and instead she drove him everyday, even though it was very inconvenient.

Ray wasn't a very tidy boy. But that didn't matter. Mom was always there to clean up behind him. If he made a mess of his room, mom would clean it up. If he broke a toy, dad would buy him a new one. They tried to get Ray to be more careful with his toys; they tried to get him to clean up his room. He was agreeable enough. But he wouldn't ever follow through.

By the time Ray was eight, his parents were growing increasingly concerned. Ray wouldn't take responsibility for any of his actions. He always blamed someone else when things went wrong. "Maybe we've smothered him too much," dad said. "Maybe we've tried to protect him so much that now he doesn't see that he needs to own up when he makes a mistake."

Mom agreed. The answer: "He'll become more responsible only if we pull away from him. Make him stand on his own two feet. If we go on protecting him, he'll never improve."

They followed through with their plan. They made Ray walk to school by himself, even though he cried and cried and asked them not to send him off alone. When he made a mistake they forced him to accept responsibility for it. They made him clean up after himself, every time. If he didn't, they'd spank him until he did. They stopped monitoring everything he did. They watched their actions, and whenever it seemed that they were protecting Ray too much, they pulled back.

It seemed like a good idea, in theory. But Ray's problem only got worse. His parents realized they needed to take another look. This time they saw their mistake. They'd been building fences for Ray, but they were either too tight or so wide he didn't even know they were there. Now they built one that was just right, and Ray improved:

Instead of making him walk to school alone, mom walked with him until he was more comfortable with going by himself.

Instead of forcing him to accept responsibility for his mistakes, his parents talked things over with him so he could understand.

Instead of spanking Ray if he failed to clean up his toys, his mom used logical consequences: when he didn't pick up a toy, she put it away where he couldn't get it.

It soon became evident that a good fence (but not too tight) was just what Ray needed. No longer was he the same clinging (and irresponsible) vine, and no longer was he feeling lost and alone. Ray was a slow developer, and it took time for him to develop self-confidence. But over the years, as he tested the fence again and again, he discovered it was strong and secure.

When Ray was assured that the fence would protect him, he began to venture out a little on his own. And gradually, slowly, he became independent and more and more responsible.

Building fences can be tricky business. If the fence is too tight, it *will* become stifling and overprotective. If it stands out too far from the child, he won't even know it's there. But if it's just right, it will make all the difference to the child's development. He'll feel safe to grow.

61

What's a Parent to Do?

Fences come in the form of family rules and limitations. As you build your own security fences, keep these ideas in mind:

- Be dependable—the fence needs to be strong.

- Involve the child in the process of setting rules—let them help build the fence.

- Let the child range around within the fence as much as he pleases.

- Make sure the fence is built in such a way that you're always there with the child, in terms of psychological support.

- As the child grows, he can venture away from the parents. But the parents should never venture away from the child.

- Don't force the child to become independent. It won't work—he'll only become more insecure—and it will strain the relations between the parent and the child.

- As the child grows, show him *how* to develop new skills.

- Be sensitive to the needs of the child. Don't get so set in your ways that you're not willing to make changes as the child needs them.

Out of the Rut and into the Groove

Here's a sure way to success: Whenever you give your child a new responsibility, make sure he gets started in it right. If he gets into a good habit with the responsibility, he'll be set in it for the rest of his life.

Patterns of responsibility—or irresponsibility—are usually hard to break. Get your child started out right in the first place. Once a child is in a good habit pattern, it makes life much easier for everyone.

It's as easy to form a good habit as a bad one. Since humans are natural habit-formers, help your child get into a good groove, not a bad rut!

When someone learns how to golf, he can do it one of two ways:

- He can learn how to hold the club wrong and ruin his golf game.

- He can learn how to hold the club right and improve his golf game.

It takes just as much energy to hold the club either way. He may as well learn how to do it right in the first place and get the benefits he wants. He may as well get into a good habit pattern right from the start.

Whenever Alice baked a ham, she cut off both ends before she put it in the oven. Jim was curious, and he asked why.

"That's the way mom always did it," Alice answered.

The next chance Jim had, he asked his mother-in-law why she cut the ends off the ham. "Oh, I don't know," she said. "That's just the way my mother always did it."

One Thanksgiving Jim and Alice invited both her mother and her grandmother to dinner. Alice cut off the ends of a ham and popped it into the oven. Jim saw his opportunity. "Grandma," he said, "Alice cuts the ends off the ham because her mother taught her that way. And mom says she learned it from you. Why do you do it—is it a religious observance or does it cook better or what?"

Grandma laughed. "No, nothing like that at all," she said. "When I was young I cut off the ends of the ham because my oven was too narrow to hold a full ham. I guess I just never got out of the habit!"

Grandma's habit ruled her actions. And, when she taught her daughter the same habit, it ruled the daughter's actions. Who knows how many generations would have been affected if Jim hadn't been so curious?

When we can get into good habit patterns with our families, life will be easier. Responsibility will flow naturally.

A bad habit is like getting into a rut. Suppose you're driving down a dirt road and suddenly your car wheels drop into a rut. You may not like it; the rut may even be taking you in the wrong direction. But ruts are hard to get out of—they hold the wheels like a vise.

You'll try to get out. But it won't be easy. Your wheels are stuck in it.

It's much better to drop into a good-habit groove than a bad-habit rut. Grooves are positive, but ruts are negative. The good-habit groove will direct your wheels too—but it will do it in the right direction.

The same thing is true of training a child in responsibility. Get him started out right in a particular duty, and he'll be able to continue in it without too much effort. The groove he's in will help him to steer.

Rut: Kids strew toys all around the house. Mother picks up after them.

Groove: Kids strew toys all around the house. But they are expected to clean them up before supper. Every night the expectation is the same, and soon the children do it automatically.

What's a Parent to Do?

The key to successful "grooving" is to set up good systems in the first place. The best place to start is in areas where there are *no* habit patterns. It's easier to drop into a groove than it is to get out of a rut.

If the children are presently in bad ruts, the parent may want to establish new systems of giving and following through on responsibility. When you do that, expect the children's behavior to get worse for a while, as they adjust. Then they'll begin to get better and better.

Here's one good groove to consider: a responsibility-reward system. If you give the child a chore to do, and he does it, he gets a reward. If he fails in his responsibility, he doesn't.

Rewards are good ways to form grooves: "If you brush your teeth, you'll get dessert tonight."

Try to create rewards that fit the situation. Say, for example, that you want you child to brush his teeth before leaving for school. That's the responsibility. The reward: healthy teeth, of course. But that's long term and will be meaningless to a child. So you offer something more immediate: "If you brush your teeth before leaving for school, you can have dessert after supper tonight. If you don't brush, no dessert." (Be sure to have the child brush after supper, too—especially if you've given him sweets! And one caution: food is an easy reward to give. But if you see *any* signs of overweight or obesity in your child, stop giving food rewards immediately! Obesity isn't a good price to pay

65

for responsibility. The attendant costs in health and self-esteem are just too great.)

Set up the rule—and then let the child govern himself. Don't nag. Don't remind. Don't fret. Doing those things is getting into a bad pattern of responsibility. Instead let the child make his own choice—and enjoy (or suffer) the consequences. If he brushes his teeth, great! He'll have healthy teeth, plus dessert! If he doesn't brush, no reward.

He'll soon get the point. And he'll learn responsibility in the process.

As the child gets older and older, he'll be able to take on more and more responsibility. He'll know that he can't lean on you when it comes to *his* responsibilities. He has to do it on his own. And he will.

But get the pattern established early. Learn early to get your child in the habit of policing himself on his responsibilities, rather than leaning on you.
If you do, he'll learn a lesson that will stay with him throughout his life.

One Way to Increase Your Chances of Raising a Responsible Child

Bill Ramsey's first child was a son, Steve. Bill was strict and undeviating with Steve, and Steve responded. He grew to be responsible and obedient.

Then Maria was born. Bill was strict with her, and she became everything he had hoped she would be.

Then along came Matt, and then Chuck. Bill was pretty set in his ways by now, and he was strict and undeviating with them. But they both rebelled, each in his turn. They wouldn't listen, and gradually the rift grew wider and wider between them.

Why? What caused the problem?

There's one thing Bill Ramsey failed to take into account: Each child is individual, a unique person, unlike anyone else in the world. **What works to build responsibility in one child may not work with another. Training methods need to be individualized, designed to match individual**

Each child is special, unique, different from every other child in the world.

children. Parents need to be sensitive to the needs of each child and adapt themselves to each different child in their family.

Individual Children Are Individuals

The variety in Sandy's family is typical. She has two girls and three boys. If she and Mark are trying to raise them all the same, they're going to be in trouble. Each child is very definitely an individual:

boy: a show-off, kind of pushy

boy: loving and caring

girl: insecure with peers

girl: reflective

boy: athletic, physically outgoing

Of course that listing indicates only one of the attributes of each child, but it conveys the idea: the dominant trait of each is very different from the others. If Sandy and Mark try to raise them all the same way, they'll probably end up with a couple of very responsible kids and a couple of rebels.

By treating each child as unique, parents show the child that he's important to them, that he is worthwhile and useful. That in turn helps the child develop feelings and characteristics that all lead to being more responsible:

- he feels more a part of the family

- he feels better about his relationships with parents and other children

- he's more willing to cooperate with others

- he recognizes the mutual trust and respect in his relationship with his parents

What's a Parent to Do?

1. Remember that each child is different. Be sensitive to the special attributes and needs of each. Childrearing approaches will vary from child to child.

2. Develop a special relationship with each child in your family. Spend quality time every week with each child, *individually*.

3. Notice the child's special interests, and help him or her build on them.

4. If things aren't going well between you and your child, the problem might be that you're trying the wrong thing—the thing that worked with the older children, or the thing that worked for your neighbor with her children. Remember your child's uniqueness and take a new tack.

5. As you try some of the ideas in this book, select the ones that go best with your child and his or her personality. Don't try to do everything; use only the ideas that fit.

A Key Factor to Becoming Responsible

Mom taught Nancy to play checkers. It was fun for both of them. Mom showed her how to make the moves, one by one. Every day they played several games, for a couple of weeks—but every time Mom took care to let Nancy win.

One day cousin Jill came to visit. "Let's play checkers," Nancy said excitedly.

"Okay," said Jill.

They started to play. Before long the game was over—and Jill had won handily. "I hate checkers," Nancy cried, knocking the board and pieces onto the floor. "I don't ever want to play again."

Learning to cope with failure and disappointment is a key factor in becoming a responsible person. Mom should have given Nancy experience with failure as well as success; she should have helped her learn how to cope with losing.

"Jack fell down and broke his crown"—everyone has a bad day now and then. The more a child can learn to cope with failure and disappointment, the more he'll be able to be responsible.

If we could structure the ideal life, we might create one without pain (though we'd be misguided if we did). But the ideal life doesn't exist, and it never will. Every one of us experiences both good and bad. Those who learn to cope with bad as well as good are the ones who learn how to be responsible when things aren't going well.

These points should put things into perspective:

- Life is full of setbacks and disappointments.

- Everyone feels discouraged at times.

- We need to learn to accept discouragement as part of life.

- Failure is one of the natural experiences of life, and a child shouldn't be sheltered from it.

- Success is simply getting up one more time than you fall down.

What's a Parent to Do?

In some ways, parents need to create situations where their children can learn responsibility. That isn't the case with failure—every child will automatically have plenty of experiences with that! The challenge is to help the child learn to cope. It's to help the child learn how to face the disappointing situations that will just naturally arise.

It's not too difficult for the average person to act responsibly when everything's going well. The challenge is to be responsible when life's falling apart. Parents can help their children maintain a steadiness in life's major catastrophes if they start early, teaching the child to cope with the disappointments of childhood.

Some thoughts:

- Don't shelter your child from failure.

- When things go wrong, encourage the child to try again.

- Show by your own example that failure in an important task isn't so important as long as you keep trying.

- Don't be afraid to give comfort, but don't overdo. Don't

make excuses for the child, and help him to avoid them, too. Instead, help him find ways to succeed.

- Let the child know that you, the parent, also make mistakes and have to redo things.
- Let him know that you also get discouraged and have setbacks but keep going anyway.

Helping the Child to Love Himself

One mother tells this story about how her son learned to respect himself more:

"One day Jimmy decided he wanted to redecorate his bedroom. I told him absolutely not. I wasn't going to let him mess up that beautiful room. I just knew he'd ruin it, and then we'd have to do it over again.

"But as we discussed it, I could tell it really mattered to him. I finally decided to let him give it a try. I don't know if I've ever seen him so excited about anything! He worked on that room every night after school for nearly a month—painting the ceiling, wall-papering, rearranging furniture, building shelves. He even stripped the old paint off his bed and put on new.

"I'll never forget the day he called me and Fred in to see his work. We could see flaws here and there, but overall he'd done a great job. Even more important, though, was the look on Jimmy's face. He was really proud of himself. He deserved to be!"

Every child needs plenty of experiences that will boost his self-esteem. **The more a person esteems himself, the more he'll hold others in esteem. And the more a person holds others in esteem, the more he'll act responsibly toward them.** It's impossible to give out something you don't have. A person can't treat others with respect if he doesn't have any *self*-respect.

Strong Enough to Care

But when someone values himself inside, he's more free to take risks. He's more able to value others, outside. How we act towards others is often a reflection of how we feel towards ourselves.

". . . the scarcest personal quality in our world today is genuine, deep, sustaining self-confidence. Look behind the

73

behavior of the bully, the egotist, the show-off, the whiner, the dictator, and you will almost always find a lack of belief in self."

J.D. Batten

The child with self-esteem:

- has a spirit of cooperation
- is little threatened by others' insecurities
- acts positively without being told
- has positive attitudes towards his family
- shares mutual respect and trust in his relationship with his parents
- has a sense of responsibility

What's a Parent to Do?

Childrearing experts agree that self-esteem is a valuable prerequisite to being responsible. But how do you instill a feeling of self-esteem in a child? It's difficult for a person to give self-esteem to himself. It comes more quickly and more powerfully if someone else sends the message of esteem.

The key is *value*—let the child know you *value* him. Try these:

- show the child he is trusted.
- provide him with success experiences.
- show in words and actions that he is a person you value.
- refuse to reward destructive behavior.
- reward positive behavior well.
- give increasingly more freedom as the child shows he can handle it.
- show your child that you value his feelings and opinions.

In all that you do, remember that the immediate results aren't as important as the effort. If a child sees that his parents are *trying* to treat him with respect, he'll automatically, gradually, increase in his feelings of self-respect.

How to Kill Responsibility Fast!

The teams hovered over the ball, their muscles tensed. The quarterback started his cadence. "Hike!" he shouted. Everyone scrambled and the fullback took off down the field, ball in hand.

He was stopped by the whistle that shrilled through the air. "Double dribble!" the referee called.

"Hey, wait a minute," said the quarterback. "This is football, not basketball!"

"Yeah," drawled the ref. "But I didn't like how things were going, so I changed the rules."

They tried again. As soon as the quarterback called "Hike!" the whistle sounded again. "You didn't say "Fore!" the referee accused.

Sometimes kids get caught in this kind of game with their parents. As soon as the kids think they have things figured out, the parents suddenly change the rules. Children can never learn responsibility when family rules change from day to day or week to week. There's nothing to be responsible *to*.

It's important that parents be as consistent as possible in how they act and react toward their children. When things are inconsistent, the child feels unstable. And instability makes the development of responsibility impossible. If responsibility already exists, it gets killed fast!

The more consistent parents are in the way they treat their children, the easier it will be for the children to become responsible. That doesn't mean we should continue to be consistent if we learn we're wrong. When changes are needed, they should be made. The goal, though, is to find the right family rules and then stick with them. Parents shouldn't be consistently wrong, but they should try to be consistently right.

The Negative Power of Inconsistency

Inconsistency teaches irresponsibility. Roger is supposed to clean his room. If he doesn't, mom informs him, he'll get punished. He knows the rule and abides by it, cleaning his room, faithfully, ten times in a row. Mom is pleased that he's doing so well.

Then one day Roger gets so busy playing that he forgets to clean his room. "Oh, well," Mom says. "He'll clean it tomorrow."

But Roger notices the inconsistency immediately. He didn't clean his room and nothing was said. *Maybe mom didn't really mean it! Maybe she's changed her mind!*

Roger decides he won't clean his room anymore, until mom makes him. Of course, mom eventually *does* take action. But she's lost a lot of ground. And Roger has backslid in learning responsibility.

Another example:

When mom puts little Tiffany to bed, she makes up her mind that she won't go back into the bedroom, no matter how much Tiffany cries. "This nightly crying has to stop!" she says to her husband, exasperated.

She's barely out the door when Tiffany begins to cry.

Tiffany cries for five minutes. Mom keeps busy on other things.

Tiffany cries for ten minutes. Mom starts to watch television, trying to ignore the crying.

Fifteen minutes. "Maybe I should see what's the matter," mom says. Dad shakes his head.

Twenty minutes. "I can hardly stand it," mom says.

After thirty minutes, mom finally gives up. She goes up to comfort her poor little baby.

That's where mom made her mistake. For thirty minutes she was consistently true to her resolve. But on the thirtieth minute she turned inconsistent and undid all of her work. And Tiffany gets the message: *If I cry long enough, mom will come up.*

Stick to Your Guns

We've seen the negative power of inconsistency. Now look at the positive power of consistency: When a particular behavior repeatedly brings the same response, the behavior tends to be perpetuated. The more a parent can be consistent in rewarding good behavior and correcting misbehavior, the more the child will get the idea—and the more he'll learn.

Which of these two lines is easier to follow—the one that's straight and true, or the one that keeps doubling back on itself, changing its mind about its direction?

"Mom says if I don't clean my room I won't get to go over to Sally's."

"Now mom says I can't go to Sally's anyway, because I didn't clear the table after breakfast."

"Mom says that if I stop whining I can play with Sally."

"I'm not sure what mom wants!"

"I stopped whining. But mom's mad at dad now. She tells me to go to my room."

"I don't know what to do! I don't feel like doing anything mom asks anymore!"

One family has a *consistent* rule that's helped the kids learn not to be sneaky. Whenever they get caught sneaking something, they end up getting less than the other kids. If Ron gets caught sneaking cookies, well: "Sorry, Ron, no more cookies for you. Come here, you other kids. I want to give you five apiece." That may seem a little harsh, but it really isn't. Because before long the kids learn that it doesn't pay to be sneaky. They've applied the rule consistently, and because of that, the kids have *learned*.

What's a Parent to Do?

If parents will establish a habit of being consistent in their actions and words, they'll find their kids becoming more responsible. Two plus two equal four, every time you add it. And increased consistency in the way parents treat their kids adds up to more responsibility, every time.

Try these:

- Make sure your kids know exactly what's expected of them.

- When you make a rule, stick by it. (That means you make rules that you *can* and *will* enforce.)

- As much as you can, consistently respond to good behavior with rewards and to bad behavior with corrections. Don't mix up the two.

- Be predictable, in the good sense of the word.

- Be consistently right, not consistently wrong.

Ignoring This Can Undo All Your Good Work

- **Johnny** broke his arm when he jumped off a shed with a towel pinned around his neck and an **S** drawn on his shirt.

- **Mary** sassed her mother when she saw a daughter on her favorite TV show get away with sassing.

- **Ruth** talked her mother into buying a cereal she saw in an advertisement because it looked so good. She swore she already loved it and would eat the whole package. (It tasted like wallboard).

- **Harold** bought some hair cream with the full knowledge that when he wore it a secret girlfriend would swoon at his feet. She didn't even notice he was alive. (But his hair stayed down well.)

- **Ron** stayed out all night cruising the main drag of his town after seeing the same thing on a popular movie.

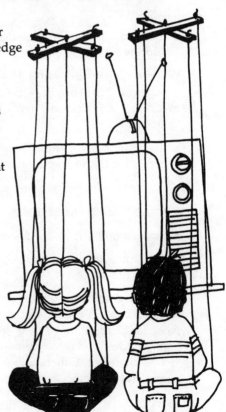

Television and other media can have a great influence on kids' behavior. And rarely do the media teach responsibility.

When you think of those examples, ask yourself: *How much are children really influenced by stories they hear, books they read, TV shows they watch, movies they go to?* There is almost always a correlation between what a kid sees and hears and what he does. The question we need to ask, then, is what are our children learning about responsibility from the media? **Children learn responsibility from role models.** The more we can influence the models they look to, the easier it will be to teach them responsibility.

Some things on television, for instance, teach the viewer:

- that sitting and watching something is often more rewarding than actively creating

- how to kill and how to dispose of the body

- how to outrun the cops in your hot car

- that commercial products can make you a beautiful person

- that being macho is more desirable than being sensitive and loving

When an impressionable child sees such things, the models often erode his sense of responsibility. But much in the media is good. Consider what a child will learn when he sees:

- that sitting down and talking through a problem is more profitable than slugging it out

- that prison life is frightening and brutal

- that helping a friend makes one feel warm inside

- that parents can be good sources of emotional help

- that things go much more smoothly when everyone does his or her share

There's a correlation between what a kid sees and hears and what he does. A parent who wants a responsible child will pay careful attention to the role models his child selects. Some models will teach immaturity, irresponsibility, and lack of character. Others will teach the opposite, and will help a child become more responsible.

What's a Parent to Do?

The key is helping the child to have good role models. If the child admires models of responsibility, half the battle is won. How can a parent influence a child's role models? A few suggestions:

1. First and foremost, be a good role model personally. Be the kind of person you'd like your child to become.

2. Influence your younger children by reading good stories to them.

3. Encourage older children to read good books and wholesome magazines.

4. Teach your children to be selective in their TV watching. At the beginning of each week, sit down together with a programming guide and decide together which shows the child may choose from. Teach them to be discriminating.

5. Monitor the movies your child goes to. If possible, preview the movie before your child sees it; or ask around to get opinions of people you trust. Even G-rated movies can be harmful—they sometimes teach principles and portray roles you may not want your child to pick up.

6. Music can have a definite effect on the psyche. It may be difficult to totally control the kind of music your child listens to—and control is almost certainly undesirable anyway. But popular music comes in varied degrees of desirability. Certain radio stations may be acceptable where others aren't, even though both play basically the same kinds of sounds.

A human being is like a computer. The old saying, "Garbage in, garbage out," is just as true with people as it is with computers. Sometimes children give their parents garbage, and fail to act responsibly, because garbage is what they're taking in. The more the parents can influence the child's intake, the better their results are going to be.

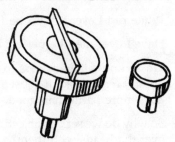

When Did You Last Meet a Perfect 10?

David is just out of high school, and he has a heck of a time pleasing his dad. He never quite measures up. Here's how the problem goes:

"David, you're such a slouch. Why don't you set some goals and improve your life?"

David wants to please dad. So he sets some goals—and they're good ones. He's done a good job.

So David takes the goals to his dad: "Look, dad. I did set some goals. I'm going to improve my life."

"Uhh! Let me look at those." Dad pauses for a moment, reading David's list. Then he hands it back. "You might as well not fool yourself. You'll never reach *those* goals!"

David's dad was expecting perfection. And he figured that if David wasn't perfect now, he never would be. (It takes a perfect person to reach high goals, doesn't it?—at least that's what David's dad is thinking).

Judging Too Harshly

Next time you find yourself judging your child too harshly, ask yourself:

When was the last time I met a perfect person?

When did I ever meet a perfect parent?

Have I ever met the perfect kid?

We all know the answers to those questions. Perfection doesn't really exist. It's just a shadowy ideal, one that often does more harm than good.

So why do we set our objectives that high, and beat our kids over the heads with them?

Children will find it easier to be more responsible if they're not burdened with perfection.

When a parent expects too much of a child, the child misses the target—and gets frustrated.

What's a Parent to Do?

Give a child a goal he can reach, and he'll be more likely to reach it. Think of how kids are at getting into things: if a child thinks he can get to the cookie jar, he'll try. But if you put it in the top cupboard, and there's no way he can climb up, and he's too small to drag a chair over, he'll leave the cookies alone. Oh, he may try a time or too, but then he'll give up.

It's the same way with progress, with perfection, with developing responsibility. If the goal is in reach, the child will go for it. Otherwise, after a feeble try or two, he'll forget it and do something else.

Some parents are always dissatisfied because nothing is perfect. They're disturbed that nobody ever measures up, either themselves or their children. They fail to recognize that imperfection is a normal, natural limitation of being human. Every parent makes his mistakes—and so does every kid.

Next time you're tempted to judge your child against the impossible standard of perfection, remember that demanding perfection—

- actually *guarantees* failure.

- doesn't allow a child to grow as he goes, which is an essential ingredient in learning.

- puts the parents out of reach of their children. They seem more powerful (deceptively so) than the child feels he can ever be.

- causes all kinds of contention between parent and child.

- causes children to fear and hate responsibility—they know that no matter how well they do on a task, it's still not good enough.

- results in a loss in the child's self-respect.

- results in an anxious child, one who's unable to perform well at just about anything.

- creates a belief that it's impossible to ever measure up. At this point some kids just stop trying altogether.

As one observer pointed out: "It's normal to spill flour when you're learning to cook; to spend your allowance foolishly when you're learning to handle money; and to be so preoccupied with whether that bully is going to beat you up that you forget to take out the garbage."

One of the Easiest Ways to Help a Child Become Responsible

- **Tara** was struggling to tie her shoelaces. Her mother watched for a minute, then sat down beside her. "Here, let mama help you," she said.

- **Dick's** father liked to be with him when he was out working in the yard. Dick was a cute kid, and it was fun to have him around. But he was too little to help, and dad wouldn't let him do anything. It wasn't long before Dick became bored and didn't want to be outside with dad anymore.

- **Janet** watched television from the time she got home from school until she went to bed. She wasn't too excited about cleaning up after herself, and her room got to be so messy that her mom finally made a habit of picking up after her.

Often it's easier to do things for a child than to get the child to do them for herself. But to take over for a child will stifle her development. The opposite approach is much more effective, and it's one of the easiest ways to help a child become responsible: **Create circumstances where the child will have to do for herself the things she's capable of doing.**

What's a Parent to Do?

Children develop gradually. They start out being able to do nothing. Then they can do a few things. Then a few more. Here's the key: as a child grows and develops new skills, require her to use those skills.

When she's old enough to tie her shoes, let her tie her shoes.

When she's old enough to clean her room, expect her to clean her room.

When she's old enough (and often kids are old enough long before their parents think they are!), she can:

dress herself
select her own clothes
make her bed
have a turn at washing the dishes
brush her teeth
wash her face
clean up her own messes
take care of a pet

As the child's abilities increase, let his or her responsibilities increase proportionately. Letting kids do things as they are able will—

- teach them self-reliance;

- build their self-esteem;

- increase their ability to do more and more things;

- help them learn how to accept responsibility.

When Children NEVER Seem to Learn

Responsibility is like a muscle: it has to be developed slowly, over a long period of time. If you exercise the muscle too much, trying to build it up too quickly, you'll suffer cramps and won't be able to work-out anymore. Or the muscle will collapse from fatigue, and you'll lose several days' exercising as you try to regain your strength.

Much better is to build the muscle slowly, little by little. Only then will you be able to make it into what you want it to be.

Try to develop responsibility in a child too quickly and the same thing will happen—he'll break down from overload, or he'll withdraw.

Much better is to build the responsibility slowly, little by little. **One of the best ways to help a child learn to be responsible is to give him practice with it.** Experience is the master teacher—a child will truly learn only when he experiences.

What's a Parent to Do?

To help a child learn how to be quiet, let him practice being quiet. Let him have experiences with it. But not all at once—the muscle takes time to develop. Perhaps the parent could start by having the child be quiet while they say grace at mealtime. Or the child could be quiet when mommy and daddy are talking during supper. Or the family can play a "Quiet Game": "Let's set the timer and see if you can go two minutes without making a sound." "Let's all be really quiet and see how many sounds we can hear." From there he can move to more extensive experiences with being quiet.

Maybe a parent wants his child to practice courtesy. He won't be courteous to everyone he meets at first—he may go up to a woman who's overweight and say, "Gee, you look FAT!" To start, parents can concentrate on smaller courtesies—saying "please," and "thank you," and "excuse me." Once the child has those down, he can move on to bigger things.

It's too much to ask a three-year-old to feed the fish. But he can learn not to unravel the entire roll of toilet paper when he uses it.

It's too much to ask a four-year-old to select all the right clothes and dress himself. But he can make a choice between two shirts you offer him, and then put on the one he picks.

It's too much to expect an eight-year-old to be able to take care of the family budget. But he can learn to handle money on a smaller scale as you give him an allowance to learn with.

Nothing drives a parent battier than a child acting like a child. But they don't know any other way. They'll develop responsible behavior only as they have practice—and even then only little by little.

The Great Responsibility Thief

Recently a small town in one of the Western states had an outstanding high school basketball team. All season long they went undefeated; they were ranked number one in the state in their class.

At the end of the year they went into the state playoffs. They were counted as the hands-down favorites. They played their first game and won by 20 points.

They went into their second game with a great deal of confidence. At halftime they were ahead by 17 points. But the other team put together a scrappy effort. By the end of the game the score was tied. After two overtimes, the favorites had lost—by one point.

The team was shattered. They had thought they were invincible. But now they learned they weren't.

The next night they went onto the court with spirits low. Their opponent was a third-place team from their region, a team they'd beaten earlier in the season. But now, instead of being confident, the team was discouraged.

Their performance showed it. They were beaten badly. And were dropped from the tournament.

Discouragement had robbed the team of their will to win. It had robbed them of their team spirit—each player ended up blaming the others for their defeat.

Discouragement generally decreases the ability to be responsible.

- The kid with a wonderful life ahead of him commits suicide.

- The girl with the high IQ gets low grades at school.

- The man with an excellent record of employment starts to do poor work and loses his job.

- A popular boy withdraws from life and becomes a social and emotional failure.

These are the extremes. But they demonstrate the point. The more discouraged a person gets, the less responsible he becomes.

Some causes of discouragement:

- little or no feedback, of any kind

- not enough positive feedback

- too much negative feedback

- goals that are set too high

- rewards that are too far in the future

Encouragement Reduces Discouragement

The way to combat discouragement is to foster
encouragement. The first thing to do is *provide success
experiences* for the child. Raymond couldn't do anything
right, it seemed. When he made his bed, he made it
wrinkled. When he washed his hands, he did the fronts
only. When he ate he missed his mouth and hit his lap.
Raymond was a prime candidate for discouragement.

But his parents embarked on a program of encouragement.
They noticed the things Ray was doing right. They praised
him for picking up his toys, even if he just dumped them in
the closet. They thanked him for coming to the dinner table
immediately when he was called—even though they
suspected his reason wasn't responsibility but famishment!

The result was that Ray felt he was worthwhile. He felt
successful in some things, and that encouraged him when
he failed in others.

Humor Softens Discouragement

One thing that will encourage a child and help her combat
discouragement is a *sense of humor*. The best source of a
sense of humor is the parent. Help the child laugh at herself
and her mistakes. And the parent can do the same with the
parent's mistakes.

Mom was trying to put together a cake. Without noticing
what she was doing, she put salt into the mixture, rather
than sugar. Then she realized what she'd done. The whole
thing was ruined—she'd have to start over.

She had several choices of how to act: she could get mad
and forget it all. She could get discouraged and forget it all.
Or she could laugh at her mistakes and try again. She
decided to have a sense of humor.

The next day Bonnie was trying to do a difficult math
problem. The teacher had given her the answer. What
Bonnie had to do was work the problem to make it come out
to that answer. Every time she tried she failed. But she
didn't get discouraged. She laughed at her mistakes and
continued on—just as she had learned many times from her
mom.

A sense of humor didn't help Bonnie do her math. But it did help her keep trying. It helped to encourage her—and it helped her to be more responsible.

The only antidote for discouragement is encouragement. And it can work every time!

Discouragement Is a Quick Road to Failure

Two high school kids were aces in tennis. They got together as a doubles team and literally became unbeatable. Every match they went to they'd blow their opponents off the court. Early in the season they were ranked as the number one team in the state—and every player throughout the state had a real fear of meeting them.

At the end of the season, these kids went to the state tournament fully expecting to win big. They advanced up through the ranks with ease. But in the quarter-finals they lost in a hard-played squeaker.

The next day they went out again to play off as runners-up. They knew the best they could do was come in third. And somewhere they lost their heart.

They played as though they had never seen a tennis racquet before. They were awkward, uncoordinated, ill-at-ease on

The more discouraged a child gets, the less likely he'll be responsible.

the court. The match was a short one, and they walked off as discouraged, confused losers.

When they were on top of the heap, they were strong players. But when they realized the couldn't win the championship anyway, the lost their desire to win. They got discouraged and played with a "don't care" attitude.

Discouragement decreases responsibility. It takes a normally responsible person and steals away his will.

What's a Parent to Do?

Parents can help their children ward off discouragement by providing them with success experiences. These experiences can come in a lot of forms, and they depend in large part on the age and stage of development the child's in. Some examples:

- Help the four-year-old learn how to tie his shoes. That will give him some success to help him deal with the defeats he has later in the day.

- Help the six-year-old have success with learning to read. Then he'll know he's not a failure in life—he can do something well.

- Help the ten-year-old do well in soccer. When he's discourage, he can go out and kick the ball around with real skill, and he'll feel better about himself.

The idea is to help the child have success in some aspect of his life. That success will give him the emotional strength to deal with his discouragements.

We shouldn't try to protect our children from failure. We couldn't do it if we tried. But if we help our children have success experiences, they'll be more able to cope with their failures. They'll still find themselves in discouraging situations, but they'll know how to deal with them without losing an attitude of responsibility.

How to Figure Out Where Your Child Stands Now

A good first step to improving a child's level of responsibility is to find out where he's starting from. How responsible is he now? Is he consistent in his behavior, or does he do some things responsibly and others not? Does he seem to be right on the verge of mature, responsible behavior, or do you have to start from scratch?

It really doesn't matter what the answers to those questions are. What matters is that the questions are asked, and that the parent learns the child's current status. **Before a parent can make progress with a child, he needs to find out how responsible the child is to start with.** The parent must work from the child's present level of development, not from the *ideal* level of development.

Take two kids. One is Little Lord Fauntleroy. The other is pure boy. Which is more responsible? It's a common tendency to equate order and achievement with responsibility—but that's not necessarily the case.

As parents make their own personal surveys, remember one important caution: *Order or achievement shouldn't be confused*

with responsibility. That's making a serious mistake, though a very common one. A child can be very orderly, having everything in its place, and still not be responsible.

The opposite is also true. Just because a child fails at something doesn't mean the child is irresponsible. He may simply have been required to perform beyond his abilities.

Maurice is a successful artist. He's at the top of his heap—by the standards of success, he's got it all. Yet it would be a great misstatement to say that he's responsible. He seems to care nothing for other people. He'll do what he must to them in order to gain his own ends. He's had several children out of wedlock, leaving both mother and child high and dry.

Successful? By all means! Responsible? Not a bit. He seems to be doing whatever he must to get more success so he can have more money to continue to be irresponsible.

This artist teaches us some important lessons:

- People with financial success aren't always responsible.

- Powerful people don't always use their power responsibly.

- Responsibility can't be measured by worldly achievement or success. One does not always equate with the other.

In seeking responsibility in your children, don't confuse some of the results of responsibility with the quality itself. Order and achievement often come to the responsible—but they're often obtained by the irresponsible as well. More important than the outward trappings of responsibility are the inward qualities of the person.

Who is more responsible—the father who works long hours to reach the pinnacle of his profession, but who never has time to play or talk with his children? Or the man who quits work at five p.m. so he can be with his family? Who is more responsible—the girl who gets good grades in school without even trying? Or the girl who studies hard and yet gets only average grades? Who is more responsible—the child who keeps his room neat and clean, yet lies about where he's been all day? Or the child who's messy at home, yet would never think of telling a lie?

What's a Parent to Do?

In trying to discover where your child presently is in terms of responsibility, ask these questions:

• Does he do what he says he will do?

• Does he seem to care about the effects his actions have on others?

• Does he respond positively to the reasonable requests you make of him?

• Does he seem to be making gradual progress in responsibility skills?

• Is he willing to accept responsibility for his own actions? Or is he prone to make excuses?

• Does he do such basic tasks as making his bed or brushing his teeth without being reminded? Does he do them once he is reminded?

• Is he able to make choices when given the chance?

• Does he get discouraged easily?

• Does he seem to have others' interests at heart—or is he consistently selfish?

Asking these questions, and making these kinds of measurements, will give a much clearer picture of how responsible a child is than will the measurements of order and success.

How to Get to the Essence of Responsibility

When Allison got up in the morning, her mom told her to wash her face. They had cold cereal for breakfast nearly every day, but Allison didn't get to choose what kinds of cereal she wanted. Her mom did the choosing for her.

Whenever mom wanted Allison to do something, she simply told her. "Clean your room, Allison. Right now." Or "I want you to run down to the store and buy some milk. Right now."

Allison felt like her mom was running her life from start to finish. One day they had a big blow-up. "You treat me like a slave!" Allison said. "I don't have any life of my own."

"Maybe you're right," mom said. "I'll try to do better." And she did try. But it soon became apparent to her that Allison had absolutely no initiative. She wouldn't do a thing unless she was told. Mom went back to her old ways.

When Allison was in junior high, her mom died. For nearly a week she sat in her room crying. She didn't go out to help her dad with meals; she didn't go to school; she didn't want to do anything. Finally her dad laid down the law: "You've got to get back into life," he said. "Starting Monday, I want you to go back to school."

Monday morning, Allison got up and went to the kitchen to have breakfast. *What shall I have?* she asked herself. She couldn't decide. Finally she settled on cold cereal, since that's what mom probably would have served. But what kind should she have?

When she got home from school, she noticed that the house was quite messy. But she couldn't quite get up and get going at cleaning it. Instead she sat down and watched television until her dad got home.

He took one look at the house and exploded. "I can't believe you're so lazy! You're absolutely unbelievable!"

Allison wasn't really lazy, and her problem with making up her mind about things didn't stem from dumbness. She'd just never had a chance to make choices. Her mom always chose for her. Or demanded.

The ability to be responsible comes from the ability to make choices. Choices are the stuff that responsibility is made of;

they are the essence of responsibility. Demands are the genesis of irresponsibility.

If a parent demands less and gives choices more, the kids will be more inclined to be responsible. Kids are just like any other kind of human being: they'd much rather feel like they're in control of their lives. When someone (namely mom or dad) makes a demand, the child feels hemmed in. He can't move around. Result: rebellion. Or, at best, *sullen* obedience. And if the child doesn't have experience with choice-making, he won't be *able* to be responsible.

Put a bridle too tightly on a colt, and you'll never train it. But put the bridle on with just the right tension, and the colt will learn to be responsive. It's all a matter of pressure. Too much pressure and you lose everything.

Kids are no different. Try this experiment. Tonight when it's bedtime, go to your kids and holler at them: "Get to bed! Right now!"

That's a demand if there ever was one—and it brings the results that demands always bring.

Next time try another approach. Don't make a demand, give a choice: "Would you like to go to bed now and have me read you a story, or would you like to play for another ten minutes and then go to bed without a story?" Or, "Would you like to go to bed and read for twenty minutes, or would you rather stay up for ten more minutes and go to bed without reading?"

Freedom of Choice Is Natural

It's natural for any living creature to seek freedom when pressure and control grows too tight. When we make demands on kids, we force them to assert their individuality in undesirable ways. Demands decrease their motivation for being responsible. Instead of obeying mom or dad for good reasons, the kid does it to stay out of trouble. Or he doesn't do it at all.

On the other hand, choices automatically bring out the good side of a kid. They allow him to assert his individuality in positive ways. You can catch more flies with sugar than with vinegar. A parent can get a lot better responses from his kids by making requests than demands.

Imagine you're watching TV and a commercial comes on. How would you respond if the announcer said, "You're required to buy this detergent. Do it now or else."

What if he said, "If you don't buy this detergent we're going to send the police after you"?

What the commercial really says, of course, is, "Here's a Brand A and here's Brand B and you can certainly buy either one you want. But you'll probably want to buy Brand A because . . ."

We like things to come to us in choices. Kids are no different.

The parent can select the area in which to give choices. Then the child can make her choices withi those limits.

What's a Parent to Do?

One of the best things a parent can do with her kids is get into the habit of offering choices. The choices should be in noncrucial things, of course, where the child can't get hurt. But too often we get into a rut of making demands, of ordering our kids around:

"Okay, time to get into bed—and I don't want any trouble!"

"I'm sick and tired of your filthy room. Clean it now!"

"If you argue with me, you're going to be grounded for two weeks!"

Probably nothing infuriates a parent more than to have her child argue with her. Why does the child argue? Because he is naturally contrary? That would rarely be the case. Instead, the child is reacting to the natural urge that all of us have to have freedom of choice.

Try to get into the habit of giving your child choices. *You* select the things to choose from, and the child gets to select which of them he wants.

If his room needs to be cleaned: "Would you like to clean your room all by yourself, or shall I help you and then you can help me with the living room?"

If he's going to a friend's house to play: "I don't want you to be gone long. Would you like to play an hour tonight, and stay home tomorrow—or would you rather play a half hour both nights?"

If it's time for bed: "I'm giving free piggy-back rides to everyone who gets pajamas on right now. Everyone one else has to *walk!*"

Offering choices develops responsibility in a very real way. As your child develops more and more the ability to make responsible choices, the time will come when he'll select his own choices, and get the job done, and you won't even have to say anything. That's when he starts to be truly responsible: when he does the right thing on his own! When that begins to happen, be sure to reward the child for choosing right.

Why "Do It My Way!" Doesn't Work

The Little Boy

Once a little boy went to school.
He was quite a little boy.
And it was quite a big school.
But when the little boy
Found that he could go to his room
By walking right in from the door outside,
He was happy.
And the school did not seem
Quite so big anymore.

One morning,
When the little boy had been in school awhile,
The teacher said:
"Today we are going to make a picture."
"Good!" thought the little boy.
He liked to make pictures. He could make all kinds:
Lions and tigers,
Chickens and cows
Trains and boats—
And he took out his box of crayons
And began to draw.

But the teacher said: "Wait!
It is not time to begin!"
And she waited until everyone looked ready.

"Now," said the teacher,
"We are going to make flowers."
"Good," thought the little boy.
He liked to make flowers,
And he began to make beautiful ones
With his pink and orange and blue crayons.

But the teacher said, "Wait!
And I will show you how."
And it was red with a green stem.
"There," said the teacher.
"Now you may begin."

101

The little boy looked at the teacher's flower.
Then he looked at his own flower.
He liked his flower better than the teacher's.
But he did not say this.
He just turned his paper over
And made a flower like the teacher's.
It was red, with a green stem. . . .

And pretty soon
The little boy learned to wait,
And to watch,
And to make things just like the teacher.
And pretty soon
He didn't make things of his own anymore. . . .

Give your child the freedom to accomplish his tasks in his own way. Parents who try to dictate not only *what* should be done but also *how* it should be done soon find themselves with a motivation problem on their hands. It's hard to be motivated to do the other person's assignment in the other person's way all the time.

Kids who get the chance to develop their own personalities and approaches, rather than being forced into a standard size or style, will be more motivated to be responsible.

"Children will readily share the responsibilities of family living, but they object to exploitation or complete disregard for their own patterns."

Francis Roberts

What's a Parent to Do?

Children grow from having experiences, not from just talking or watching. Failures teach as much as successes. Through experiences, both good and bad, a child will learn the best way to do a task. And in the process, the child will develop responsibility—he'll be learning *by his own experience* that "if a job is worth doing, it's worth doing well."

When parents give their kids responsibilities around the house, they should let the kids decide *how* the job will be done. All the parent should be concerned about is whether or not the mission is accomplished, not the means the child used to get there.

Rob has the job of washing the dishes three nights a week. Mom should stay out of his hair and let him do it. Maybe he's not as efficient and fast as she is, but that doesn't matter. All that matters is that the job gets done, meaning there are clean dishes to eat from the next day.

Betty is supposed to keep the lawn watered during the summer. Dad shouldn't tell her when to turn it on and when to turn it off (unless her assignment is to turn the water on and off, which is a different thing). Let Betty take care of it—all that matters is that the lawn doesn't turn brown and die.

And never, ever, do a job over when the child's done. If the child has done such a poor job that the chore has to be redone, let the child redo it!

Too much supervision in giving out assignments will result in loss of independent thinking and creativity. Before long, parents might find they've created a batch of unthinking robots, who are exact replicas of mom and dad—all the way down to the unhappy imperfections.

He Did It Their Way

Look at how the little boy ended up in the poem we started with:

. . . Then it happened
That the little boy and his family
moved to another house,
In another city,
And the little boy
Had to go to another school. . . .

And the very first day
He was there,
The teacher said:
"Today we are going to make a picture."
"Good!" thought the little boy,
And he waited for the teacher
To tell him what to do
But the teacher didn't say anything.
She just walked around the room..

When she came to the little boy
She said, "Don't you want to make a picture?"
"Yes," said the little boy.
"What are we going to make?"
"I don't know until you make it," said the teacher.
"How shall I make it?" asked the little boy.

"Why, anyway you like," said the teacher.
"And any color?" asked the little boy.
"Any color," said the teacher.
"If everyone made the same picture,
and used the same colors,
How would I know who made what,
And which was which?"
"I don't know," said the little boy.
And he began to make a red flower with a green stem.

Helen E. Buckley

Ten Easy Rules for Raising a Delinquent

1. Begin at infancy to give the child everything he wants. In this way he will grow up to believe the world owes him a living.

2. When he picks up bad words, laugh at him. This will make him think he's cute.

3. Never give him any spiritual training. Wait until he is 21, and then let him "decide for himself."

4. Pick up everything he leaves lying around—books, shoes, clothes. Do everything for him so that he will be experienced in throwing all responsibility on others.

5. Quarrel frequently in his presence. In this way he will not be too shocked when the home is broken later.

6. Give a child all the spending money he wants. Never let him earn his own. Why should he have things as tough as you had them?

7. Satisfy his every craving for food, drink, and comfort. Denial may lead to harmful frustrations.

8. Take his part against neighbors, teachers, policemen. They are all prejudiced against your child.

9. When he gets into real trouble, apologize for yourself by saying: "I never could do anything with him."

10. Prepare for a life of grief. You are bound to have it.

Developed by the Houston Police Department

The Best Thing a Parent Can Do

One of the best things parents can do for their kids is believe in them. Children reach for the expectations their parents set for them. What if the parents don't set very high expectations? The child ends up with a low level of performance. On the other hand, parents who believe in the unique potential of each of their children usually end up with kids who excel. And they end up with kids who are responsible in every sense of the word.

Children can believe in themselves when they know that somebody else believes in them. When they believe in themselves, they're more able to do the things their parents want them to.

When parents show their kids they believe in them, the kids are likely to do all they can to live up to the expectations."

When dad shows he believes in his son, the son is more apt to believe in himself.

What's a Parent to Do?

Okay, so we should show our children that we believe in them. How do we do that?

Try these:

1. Show the child you see him as capable. Give him chores and tasks around the house. Make sure the task is adapted to his age and ability, and that he understands what's expected. *Then let him alone while he does it.*

2. Show your child that he makes an important contribution to the family. *Listen* to him when he talks to you. Let him participate in family activities, even if it seems he's too young for them. Help him have success experiences with other members of the family.

3. In your daily expressions, show the child that you trust him and know he can do what's needed. Which parent conveys a belief in his child:

"Judy, if you don't have that mess cleaned up in five minutes, you're going to really get whacked!"

"Judy, thanks for making your bed this morning. Now help me clean up this mess, and then we can make lunch together."

Edison's Mother

The story of Thomas Edison shows us how vital parental support is. When Tom was eight he was enrolled in a one-room school. The teacher was a strict parson—and the parson didn't take long to demonstrate his methods: failure to learn was met with a stiff leather strap.

Thomas Alva didn't respond to the stiff leather strap. Within three months he was at the bottom of his class. The teacher called him "addled"—and Tom began to believe him. He felt he was a dunce and a failure.

In steps a supportive mother. Nancy Elliot Edison pulled her son from the school and determined to teach him herself. Every morning, as soon as the day's housework was done, Nancy sat down with Tom and coached him in his three Rs.

Nancy didn't do a great deal with Tom's intellect—he had plenty of innate ability there, and he didn't need much help. But she did help him in another, more important, way: *she showed her son that she believed in him.* The whole world can see the results of that belief.

When Children Don't Finish What They Start

Brian needed to get his car painted. He checked with one of his acquaintances, Ralph, to see if he could help him. "Sure," Ralph said. "You sand it and get it ready and I'll paint it for you."

Brian went to work. He rented an electric sander and took off the rough spots. He put on a primer coat over the bare spots. Finally he had the car ready. He took it over to Ralph's.

"I'll have it ready for you by the end of the week," Ralph said.

"Great!" Brian replied. "We're going on a trip next week and that will be perfect."

Brian called back on Friday. "I'll have it done by tomorrow night," Ralph said.

On Saturday night Brian stopped by. The car was half painted. Ralph was gone. "He had to run a couple of errands," his wife said.

The next week Brian took the car on his trip, half painted. He was real proud to drive around in a car like that! He never could get Ralph to finish the job. Finally he had to take it to a car shop. He ended up paying more than he would have in the first place.

Children who can learn to finish what they start will find it easier to learn to be responsible. Sometimes they'll bite off more than they can chew. Sometimes they'll lose interest halfway through a project. But if they can follow-through and finish, it will benefit them in every part of their lives.

Some things aren't worth finishing. But, with those, it's better not even to begin.

Children should
be taught to finish
what they start.
When they learn
otherwise, they
learn
irresponsibility.

What's a Parent to Do?

Parents can help by emphasizing finishing to their children.
"I know you can't do everything in the world. But what you
decide to do, and what you agree to do, I'll expect you to
finish."

It's better to have lower goals, and finish what you start,
than it is to have higher goals and never finish anything.

Jennifer has struggled with this all her life. When she was
young she took piano lessons. They were fun, and when
she got better, she talked her mom into buying her a stack of
sheet music. One by one she started to learn new songs,
enthusiastic and excited. Things always started out well. But
before she got to the end of each song, she'd bog down.
Finally she'd give up and move on to another song.

She says she can play 187 introductions but not a single
complete song!

Luckily, she's since learned to finish what she starts. The
more parents can help their children finish what they start,
the more responsible the children will become.

One Important Thing to Remember about Kids

Kids—

- want to identify themselves with adults.
- do what they think is grown up.
- like responsibility.
- imitate parents or other adults they admire.
- may misbehave at home and then act quite grown-up in public.
- may do their best to act grown-up in every way . . .

But they're **still** kids!

Kids may do all sorts of things to look like adults. But, deep down inside, they'll still just kids.

Kids are kids—they're not just small adults. They will imitate adults for a while, but they can't keep the effort up for long. And they shouldn't be expected to. After all, how can an eight-year-old know how to act like an eighteen-year-old? He hasn't been there. And he won't be for ten years!

Acting Their Age

One day Wendy's kids were really acting up. "Why can't they just act their age?" she said to her husband. But even as she said it she realized her mistake: they *were* acting their age. Two-year-olds act like two-year-olds. Oh, they may be "mature" for a while and act like three-year-olds, or even like someone even older. But only for a while. Then the situation changes and suddenly the kid is acting his age again.

What's a Parent to Do?

Once we get this idea into our minds, it makes a difference in how we act with our kids. We want them to be responsible, and we want it *now!* But, since they're just kids, we can't have it. We have to take it a step at a time, and let the kids grow into it. That's the only approach that will work.

That doesn't mean that parents have to tolerate every little thing a kid does wrong, just because he's a kid. Kids *can* be quiet, at least for a while. Kids *can* eat without spilling their food, at least when they reach age three or four. Kids *can* make their bed every day, at least when they're old enough to reach. But parents should remember, even while they're training and hoping and encouraging and teaching, that kids are kids. To expect anything else is to be unrealistic.

How to Increase a Child's Desire to Be More Responsible

Imagine this one-way dialogue—and how you'd react to it:

"Jones, you've worked well for this company several years now, and we've appreciated your efforts. Now we need you to move your family to this other city a thousand miles away—I can't really tell you where; that would only confuse you. We don't have a branch there or anything, and you may be wondering why I'm sending you there. Well, you wouldn't understand anyway.

"Now, I don't want to hear any ifs, ands, or buts. If you want to be a member of this company, you'll *just do it!*"

It doesn't take a lot of imagination to figure out how we'd feel if our bosses approached us that way. And that's exactly how kids often feel, when their parents approach them that way. "I want you to do this and don't ask why because you wouldn't understand anyway—*just do it!*"

Explaining to a child why he is to be responsible helps to increase his desire to be responsible.

Speaking the Language of Emotion

Younger children almost invariably base their decisions on emotion. They don't have a lot of logical ability. When a parent gives a reason for a desired action, then, the reason should be emotionally based.

Then, as the child grows, he'll gradually develop the ability to think and reason things through. At the same time, the parent can gradually appeal to logic as well as to emotion.

What this means is that it's not enough for a parent to give a reason for being responsible. The reason has to be one that the child can understand and appreciate. An adult's reason may not be a reason at all to a child.

The parent may say, "Don't go out into the street. Cars go fast and one might hit you." That's logical. But with a child young enough to be warned that, it probably isn't enough. The parent needs to add on a little *feeling:* "The car might hit you and you'll get hurt!" Hurt is something a child can understand.

A father tells his son to put the shopping cart in the shopping cart stall in the parking lot. He doesn't give any reasons—and the son, accordingly, isn't very responsible. The boy pushes the cart over toward the stall, then shoves it in the general direction of the stall and leaves it.

"No, son," the father explains. "We need to actually stick it inside the stall. If we don't, it might roll and hit a car and dent it or chip the paint."

Ah! Now the son understands and he does the job right.

Reasons for Helping

One summer Robert needed some help with the yard, and he asked Steve, his oldest son, to pitch in. Steve immediately started a fight. "I don't want to help in the yard. I didn't mess it up. I've got other things to do."

So then Robert explained the reasons: "The yard is for the whole family. You like to play out there as much as the younger children. It's no fun to play out there when the grass is scraggly and there are papers strewn around. If we don't do it now, it will be much harder to clean up next week."

Suddenly Steve *understood*. The fight left him. "Okay," he said. "Let's get busy."

Before he had all kinds of reasons *not to be responsible*. Now he'd been given some reasons to be responsible. It made all the difference. Of course, kids won't always make an immediate turn-around when we begin explaining. But it's a place to start. An important one.

What's a Parent to Do?

So you ask your child to do something, and he doesn't respond. What's the next step? Most of us have habit patterns to tell us where to go from this point:

"You do it RIGHT NOW!"

"If you don't get with it, I'm going to give you the spanking of your life!"

"All right! No work, no supper!"

"You're just a brat. I can't trust you do to anything right. Guess I'll have to do it myself. *Again!*"

But those habits don't bring the results we want. Sure, the work may get done, but the child hasn't learned anything. The next time we want him to be responsible, we have to go through the same old thing again.

Try this instead. Try explaining to the child:

- Tell the child how he'll feel if he doesn't do the responsible thing. Speak the language of emotion.

- Tell the child how he'll feel if he *does* do the responsible thing.

- Tell the child how you'll feel if he does or doesn't choose to be responsible. Again, the language of emotion.

- Explain things logically. As the child grows older and older, he'll understand this more and more. *But never rely on this totally. Even mature adults are more motivated by their emotions than by their understandings!*

Telling a child not to play in the street may not do much good. But explaining how cars go fast and can't stop in time might help the child understand.

An Important Tip about Teaching Responsibility

Suppose you're teaching a child how to ride a bike. Do you put her on and say, "Good luck"? Not if you want her to learn quickly and with a minimum of scrapes. Instead, you start small and easy and work up. For instance, you may take these steps, though you may not even think about it:

Step 1: Show the child how to get on.

Step 2: Show her how to steer while you push.

Step 3: Show her how to brake the bike.

Step 4: Show her how to coast downhill, solo.

Step 5: Show her how to peddle while she goes downhill.

Step 6: Show her how to peddle while she's on level ground, combining all her skills together.

It's easy to see if you're pushing the child too fast. It's easy to see if you're trying to get her to do things she's not ready for. And when that's the case, you simply continue with the step she's on until she's ready for the next one. By going step by step, you're able to convey the ideas and skills to the child, until gradually she's able to do the whole thing.

The same thing is true of teaching responsibility. **Most new responsibilities are best learned by starting the child with something small and easy and working progressively to bigger and harder things.** Give the child too much at once and you'll end up discouraging and defeating him. You'll overload his system, and he'll be unable to accomplish anything at all. But give him a little and let him master that before giving him more, and he'll end up a master of the situation.

To have order in a home requires that kids help in household chores. Kids need to feel, too, that they're contributing to the smooth workings of the household. Even younger children can participate in such responsibilities—if the parent gives them just a little to start with. Then, gradually the child can be given more and more to do.

Little by little, the child will be gaining skill and confidence—and a sense of responsibility.

Home Cooking

Suppose mother does all the cooking. Her seven-year-old can be given some of the responsibility to help. Mom can pick out the menu for the day and give the child a simple recipe to follow. As the child grows older, mom can give her more and more to do—until the child plans the menu, buys the ingredients, and cooks the meal.

The family likes to go on periodic outings. Instead of dad planning everything, he can give the children assignments to help. As they get older, they can take turns deciding where to go and what to do. The older children can even make reservations, plan itineraries, and so forth.

Little things done well lead to big things done well. As the child gains confidence and skill. The child will thus be able to go through a chain of successful experiences in being responsible. With each new assignment he'll gain more self-confidence and maturity.

What's a Parent to Do?

The key to building responsibility in a child is to start small and work up. Helping a child learn responsibility isn't a one-time thing, nor does it happen automatically. He needs to be taken step-by-step. If he backslides, the parent must carefully help him back into the path of progression.

Remember that responsibility is progressive. It doesn't happen overnight. Let a child master one point, then he'll be ready for the next.

A good sequence to help the child learn:

- Select the task you want the child to learn. If possible, choose something where mistakes don't matter. It also helps if the results of the job are visible, so the child can see his improvement.

- Break the task into steps.

- Isolate the steps and teach them one at a time.

- Allow the child to master and remember each step before moving on to the next one.

- Once the child has learned all the steps, check him to see if he's assimilated the learning and to see if he can combine the steps to accomplish the overall task.

Isolate the steps of a task, and the child won't feel the whole world crushing down on him at once. After he masters the first step, isolate the second step, and let him learn it.

How to Use Punishment That Brings Results

One expert put it nicely: "Sometimes the quickest way into a kid's brain is through his bottom."

Three-year-old Jill is playing out in the street. It's not a real busy street but who knows when an inattentive motorist might come by? Mom rushes out and swoops Jill back onto their lawn. Time for a spanking, to reinforce the message that mom has already repeatedly taught: "You do *not* go out into the street for any reason!"

Mom could sit and reason with Jill all day about the dangers of going into the street—but a swift spanking gets the message across much quicker and much more effectively.

Sometimes punishment is the best way to change irresponsible behavior. That doesn't mean the parent has to spank all the time. There are other forms of punishment, including logical and natural consequences, which we discuss in another section. (See "Give 'Em What They Deserve!") But still the punishment often has to be immediate and sure.

Sometimes an approach through the kid's bottom . . .

. . . is the quickest way to his brain.

119

Here are some keys to effective punishment:

- **Make teaching and training the mainstays of your approach.** It's the teaching and training you do that will help the child grow and develop, not the punishing. Punishment brings only temporary results.

- **Use physical punishment only as a last resort.** Logical and natural consequences are better ways of bringing change.

- **Be firm as well as kind.** By being firm you show that your point-of-view must be respected. By being kind you indicate that you recognize the child also has a point-of-view.

- **Be consistent.** When you decide on a course of action, stick to it. Don't vacillate back and forth. But seek to be consistently right, not consistently wrong.

- **Exercise self-control.** Don't punish in anger, but in love. Give the punishment because you view it as a teaching tool, not because you're upset at your child.

- **Issue a warning first.** Before you ever punish, make sure the child knows the rule. If the child misbehaves after that, apply a mild form of punishment. If the mild punishment doesn't bring results, discipline more severely. (But never apply physical punishment to the point where it will harm the child. That's child abuse, not discipline. The same applies for emotional punishment.)

- **Administer the punishment immediately after the misbehavior.**

- **Make the punishment relate to the misbehavior.** If possible, use discipline to teach rather than simply to change behavior.

- **Make the punishment correspond to the seriousness of the offense.** As one teacher put it, don't use a howitzer when a pea shooter will handle the job.

- **After punishing, make an opportunity to reaffirm your love to the child.**

You Say Your Kids Won't Do Their Work?

Brad and Allen were *supposed* to be cleaning their room. The key word there is *supposed:* it was getting messier by the minute. When they started, there were dirty clothes all over the floor; papers from school were under the mussed blankets on the bed, under the bed, under the dresser, and on the window sill; drawers of the dresser were hanging open.

But that was only the beginning. Now the drawers were empty, and the clean clothes were mixed in with the dirty ones, scattered all over the floor. Brad had found one of his sneakers—and proceeded to dump the sand in it out into his pillowcase.

And that was only the beginning. . . .

What's a mother to do!?

The problem is that Brad and Allen weren't given a very good reward for cleaning their room. In fact, the *only* reward was that they'd have a clean room. Pretty exciting for a four and six year old, huh!

So now their mom tried to give a good reward: "Brad, Allen—as soon as your room is clean, I'll give you a snack!"

Magic!

The more kids are encouraged and rewarded for doing the right thing, the more they'll want to do it. Want your kids to be responsible? Give them rewards for being responsible. But there's a catch. You can't at the same time give "rewards" for things you don't like them doing. That will confuse them—and mess up your life.

Raising Good Fruit or Good Kids

Think of the fruit trees some people like to plant in their backyards. If they just stick them there and don't give them

121

any encouragement to grow, they won't do very well. In fact, if there isn't much rain in that area, the tree will probably die.

But if they encourage that tree, "reward" it, it will take off. They'll need to water it periodically, put fertilizer around the roots, prune it, spray the bugs—and then it will bear lots of good fruit.

A child is the same as a tree. The more good attention you give him, the better fruit he'll bear.

Plant an apple tree and encourage it to grow with water and fertilizer and you'll end up with some nice fruit.

Take a child and encourage her to grow with meaningful attention and she'll give you some good fruit.

Rewards

Here are some rewards a parent can try:

- smiling
- praise
- doing things together
- more responsibility
- a touch, a hug, a kiss
- recognition
- money
- attention (good kind)
- food
- more freedom
- special privileges

These are just to get you started. There are lots more rewards you can try. The idea is to give the child something he'll like, and to connect the giving to responsible behavior.

What's a Parent to Do?

As you use rewards in your family, keep these ideas in mind:

- Be sure to give rewards for good behavior, not simply for "Being good." Being good can be an absence of bad behavior, while good behavior means that the child is *doing* something. Some parents seem to think the optimal state in kids is constant quietness, which is obtainable only from a frontal lobotomy. They reward accordingly. That doesn't teach responsibility, but only passiveness.

- Make sure that what you're giving is a reward to the child. "John, as soon as you get your work done, I'll take you over to Aunt Mabel's house to play with cousin Rob." Maybe that would seem like a great reward to the parent, but to the kid it might be a punishment. Aunt Mabel is stern and demanding and Rob is a selfish little snot!

How to Make the Right Things Happen

Extremes in parenting styles don't seem to work. Raising a kid is like flying a kit. If you pull in on the string too much, the kite won't have any freedom to fly higher. You'll hold it down.

But if you let the string go too loose, the kite will lose its flying power and fall to the ground. Or, in the greatest extreme, you let go of the string and the kite flies away and you won't have it anymore.

Parents need to maintain control on their kids like they would on a kite. They should be neither too strict nor too permissive, neither too hard nor too soft. The middle approach is the only way to really be successful.

And only with the moderate approach will the child have the freedom he needs to learn how to be responsible.

The difference is like that between the Authoritarian and the Libertarian. The Authoritarian, at one end of the scale, says, "If you don't do what I say, you're going to catch heck!"

At the other end of the scale, the Libertarian says, "Oh, what the heck! Do what you want!"

Neither the Libertarian or the Authoritarian is going to raise a responsible child. (If he does, it will be pure luck!) Because with the Authoritarian parent the child doesn't ever have an *opportunity* to be responsible on his own. And with the Libertarian parent the child doesn't ever have any *motivation* to act responsibly on his own.

What's a Parent to Do?

How do you know that you're using the right parenting style? It's easy to tell. If the child knows that he's loved and respected, consistently, the parenting style is a good one. If the child doesn't know those things, the parenting probably needs to change.

It may help to ask yourself a few questions:

Am I an Authoritarian?

Do I fly off the handle if my child doesn't jump immediately when I say jump?
Do I find myself quickly spanking when my child is irresponsible?
Does my child hear me yelling as much as he hears me talking nicely?

Am I a Libertarian?

If my child doesn't do what he's supposed to, do I end up doing it for him?
Do I allow him to talk back to me?
Do I pretty much let him have his way in order to avoid a scene?

Am I a good mixture of the two?

Am I firm but loving when I require my child to do things?
Do I expect my child to be responsible, and take the steps to promote it through teaching and effective persuasion?
Am I willing to punish when necessary, but try to use punishment to teach and correct rather than to give him what he deserves?

Extremes in parenting styles are common, but they simply don't work. Oh, both kinds of parents get what they want for now: The Authoritarian gets the job done. The Libertarian avoids hassle. But, over the long haul, both fail. In both cases the child fails to gain responsibility for himself and his own actions.

Only when the parents find a good middle ground between the extremes will the child really reach his potential as a responsible human being.

"I Never Get No Respect!"

The more you respect something, the more you'll act responsibly toward it. This is as true for kids as it is for adults. If a child doesn't respect something, he won't be responsible toward it. If he does respect it, he values it more, and he'll be more responsible.

The idea is to get kids to respect their parents. Then the kids will be more responsible—they'll be more willing to behave the way they *should* behave.

But respect is a two-way street. The best way to get it is to give it. If a parent wants his child to respect him more (and therefore be more responsible), the parent must first respect the child more.

respect (ri-spekt) v., to hold in high regard, to esteem.

Nonrespect Versus True Respect

A good example is how a parent deals with the problem of getting a child to do his homework. One approach is to nag the child, keep close tabs on him, check up on him, constantly follow-up. This is the *non*respect approach—it tells the child that you don't trust him to be responsible with his homework.

The second approach is to let the child shoulder the responsibility for the homework. Let it be an issue between him and his teacher, with you as parent becoming involved hardly at all—except to give approval and praise when he does it and does it well. If you start your child in school with this attitude, he'll know from the beginning that the homework is his responsibility, not yours. He'll know that you respect him, that you trust him to do it on his own.

126

If you've been checking up on homework, you may have a little more difficulty in instituting this approach. Don't despair, though: let your child know of your new attitude and then stick with it. Soon enough he'll recognize that you do respect him, and he'll respond accordingly.

"There is no escape from the fact that **a child learns what he lives.** *If he lives with criticism, he does not learn responsibility. He learns to condemn himself and find fault with others. He learns to doubt his own judgement, to disparage his own ability, and to distrust the intentions of others. And, above all, he learns to live with continual expectation of impending doom."*

Haim Ginott

"I respect you. That makes me want to be more responsible."

"I respect you. I trust you to make the right decision."

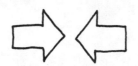

Respect is a two-way street. When a parent offers it to a child, the parent is apt to get more of the same back.

What's a Parent to Do?

People treat others differently when they respect them. By their very actions they say, "I trust you. I respect you." Here are some actions parents can try to *show* respect to their children:

- give them the right to express their feelings
- give them space to *be*
- let them have control over what they're able to control
- refrain from using force to get them to do something

- show trust by letting them make their own choices and
  decisions in appropriate situations

- *listen* to them when they have something to say

This kind of respect works like a charm. When you respect a
child, you don't interfere with things that are his
responsibility. When you don't interfere, he quickly gets the
idea that the responsibility *is* his—and he'll soon take over
on his own.

> "What is wrong with our homes? Wherein does the weakness
> lie; may we ask from whence will come the strength to cope
> with the problems? Such strength as we will muster can only
> come from within—within the individual, within the family.
> Such strength can only come by being solidly bound together
> by love and respect of the child for the parent and parent for the
> child, and the love of husband and wife. The home is the place
> to build such strength."
>
> John H. Vandenberg

A Way to Make Teaching Responsibility Easier

"One day I yelled at David to make his bed and clean up his room before he left for school. But when I finished the breakfast dishes, he was gone and the mess was still there. I was furious. I kept thinking about it all day, becoming more and more angry.

"The moment David got home I told him he wasn't going anywhere until he did his chores. He'd looked happy and eager to tell me something when he came in, but I never gave him a chance to say a word. He got very quiet, did what he was supposed to and went out without a word.

"An hour later his sister came home and said, 'Isn't it wonderful about David?' It seems he'd won a city-wide contest for the best composition on 'Why the United Nations Is Important to Me.'' That was what he'd wanted to tell me when he walked in. I lost a precious moment of excitement and happiness with my child for a lousy unmade bed!"

Eda LeShan, *Woman's Day*, Nov. 25, 1980

Having a good relationship with a child is almost always more important than teaching or enforcing responsibility. Before a parent can hope to instill attitudes of responsibility in a child, the parent and child must first develop a good relationship. If the relationship isn't there, an inward feeling of responsibility won't be there. People must always matter more than the *things* around them.

And never, never, make a relationship contingent upon responsible behavior. The relationship comes first. If a parent can establish with the child that she loves the child no matter what the child does, the child will be more likely to try to do what the parent likes.

Good relationships help make teaching responsibility easier.

129

What's a Parent to Do?

Trust, acceptance, and understanding are essential to a good relationship. That means the parent must accept the child's *efforts*, as well as his successes. Here are a few suggestions on how to make it work:

- Recognize that the child's performance may not always be up to adult standards.

- Don't set standards so high that no child could ever meet them.

- Recognize that the result isn't nearly as important as the effort.

- Be careful not to undercut both the relationship and the child's self-esteem by redoing a job behind the child.

- Try to see things from the child's point of view to increase understanding.

- Spend good time each day building the relationship between you and the child, with no thought of responsibility.

If a parent and child don't have a good relationship, the child won't be too motivated to act responsibly. But if the relationship has been firmly established to start with, the child will want to act responsibly to maintain the relationship.

How to Really Get Children Going

> "Cheshire-Puss," . . . said Alice, "would you tell me, please, which way I ought to go from here?"
>
> "That depends a good deal on where you want to get to," said the Cat.
>
> "I don't much care where—" said Alice.
>
> "Then it doesn't matter which way you go," said the Cat.
>
> "—so long as I get *somewhere*," Alice added as an explanation.
>
> "Oh, you're sure to do that," said the Cat, "If you only walk long enough."
>
> Lewis Carroll, *Alice's Adventures in Wonderland*

The cat's point was well taken. If a child doesn't really know where she wants to go, she won't have a lot of purpose in her traveling. It won't matter which direction she goes, or how fast.

Having a sense of purpose helps to increase responsibility. The more a child knows what she's up to, and why, the more diligent she'll be in an effort to get there.

Aimless people aren't responsible people. They need to get a sense of direction. They need to know who they are and where they're going. Children can be aimless as much as anyone else. But setting and accomplishing goals can make the difference: it can give the child a direction, a sense of purpose.

Goals will get a child going like nothing else can!

The Spelling Bee

Ten-year-old Nancy set a goal to win a spelling bee. She worked hard at it. The goal made her responsible—she really wanted to reach it. Every night she'd pore over her lists, studying the way the words were put together. She practiced with her older brothers and sisters. When the spelling bee was finally held, the family members weren't surprised at all when she came out at the head of her class.

131

We've all seen how purposeful a little child can be when he really wants something. Two-year-old Mike was building a tower with hook-together blocks. He wanted it to be as tall as he was. The only problem was that the blocks weren't really sturdy enough to go that high—at least that's what his parents thought.

But that didn't deter Mike. He had a purpose. And he stuck with the task until he accomplished his goal.

Parents Can Help

Parents can help a child set goals by showing how they can be broken down into smaller objectives. For instance, Larry wanted a new bike. It cost $125, which seemed almost impossible to save. To help him, his mom figured out how much each part of the bike cost: the frame, the wheels, the tires, the brakes, the chain, the handlebars, the hand grips, the fenders, and so forth. Then she helped him begin to save for an item at a time. After a few months, Larry had been able to save for the entire bike.

In the same way, parents can use smaller objectives to reach larger goals with their children. Randy never cleaned his room. And that's no exaggeration. His mom fretted and stewed and tried one ineffective method after another. Nothing worked.

Finally mom decided to break her larger goal (a clean bedroom) into smaller objectives. Instead of trying to get Randy to clean his whole room, she concentrated on one task at a time. For a whole week, all he had to do was reach the smaller objective. Her plan of attack went like this:

First week: pick up clothes and put in hamper.

Second week: pick up toys and put on shelf. Continue to pick up clothes.

Third week: make bed. Also pick up toys and clothes.

Fourth week: straighten clothes in drawers. Also make bed and pick up toys and clothes.

The training period took some time. But, step by step, Randy got into the habit of cleaning his room. By breaking the larger goal into smaller objectives, mom was able to help Randy become more responsible.

What's a Parent to Do?

Goals give a purpose and direction to life. The more a child has goals, the more purpose he'll have. And when he has a purpose, he'll be responsible for those things he's interested in.

Here are some ways to help a child set goals:

- Distinguish between goals and objectives. Goals are lofty and timeless and unmeasurable. Objectives are specific and measurable. Objectives often have a time period attached to them. Goals are the top of the flight of stairs you want to climb; objectives are the steps that take you to the goal.

- When he's faced with a challenge, help him establish some short-term goals that will help him to meet it. Help him break the task down into smaller pieces—the objectives.

- Periodically sit down with her and help her learn how to establish long-term goals. These should be suited to the age and interest of the child. The parent can make suggestions, but there should be no pressure for the child to accept them. The long-term goals of a six-year-old might look into the future for only a year; a twelve-year-old might set goals three years away, or even farther.

- Encourage the child to put both the goals and objectives down in writing. Help with the writing if your child is too small.

- Regularly go over the objectives with your child to see how he is doing with them. The child doesn't have to answer to you for his own goals or objectives, but a review will help him see for himself where he stands.

A Way to Get Kids Saying "Yes!"

"I went in to work one morning and my boss said, 'Good morning. I want you to do this and here's how to do it and here's when it's to be done and if you don't do it exactly right it won't work out and—oh, heck, I might as well do it myself!'

"My boss made three big mistakes. The first was that he didn't allow me to participate in deciding how to do the job. The second was that he ended up doing it himself. And the third was that in the process he totally destroyed my self-esteem, at least for that day.

"The result of all that: I didn't feel as much like being responsible in the company."

The more a child participates in deciding what he'll be responsible for—and how—the more involved he'll tend to get. And the more involved he is, the more responsible he'll end up being. A parent will get more support from his children if he lets them give input into deciding what's to be done, and when and how.

"Children learn rules by helping to make them."
Francis Roberts

Let a child participate in the decisions that affect his life, and he'll be more likely to say "yes."

What's a Parent to Do?

Here are some ways this idea can be applied:

134

The child's room.

Let the child participate in decisions about his room. "Which of these three pictures would you like in your room? Would you like your picture on this wall or this other one? Would you like your bed here or over here? Which day of the week would you like to vacuum the room? Would you rather keep your toys on a shelf or in a box?" Older children can help with the decoration of the room, selecting paint or wallpaper and helping to put it up.

The child's clothing.

Parents know how much they have to spend on their children's clothing, and they know which items of clothing the kids need. But the kids can participate in selecting the clothes. "Which of these pants would you like better? We can afford this dress or this one—which would you like us to get? Would you like pajamas or a nightgown?" In some families, older children are given a monthly allowance to spend on clothes; they can spend it any way they like.

The child's food.

Food is another area where parents can let the child participate in decisions, and thus develop more responsibility. It probably wouldn't be a good idea to ask the child what he wants for breakfast. What if he answers "steak and eggs"? Or what if he says "candy bars"! But you can give the child choices: "Do you want cold or hot cereal? Do you want your bread toasted or plain? Would you rather have bacon or sausage with your eggs?" Older children can help fix breakfast on certain days of the week.

Family decisions.

One good place to let children participate in family decisions is at a family council meeting. These are best held regularly, with the whole family involved. Family council doesn't mean democracy—the kids choose between options that the parents select. But as the kids get a chance to participate in decisions that will affect them, they'll become more responsible in the family.

And the family council will give the parents a chance to evaluate how their kids are doing.

The Best Way of All to Teach Responsibility

Marian tied a post to a little tree, to help it grow straighter. Her effort worked: as the years went by that tree grew straight and tall.

When the tree was big enough she took the post down. Now there was no chance of the tree growing crooked. It didn't need the post to point it upwards anymore.

The first big wind that came along blew the tree down. She had made the tree straight, sure—but in the process she'd made it dependent on the post. Without the post it couldn't stand when things got rough.

Sometimes parents want their kids to be totally dependent on them. Dependent kids are often very well-behaved, and they have all the trappings of being responsible.

But the kids are only giving the appearance of being responsible. **Dependency doesn't create responsibility. It only creates dependency.** That means when mom and dad are gone, the dependent child doesn't really know what to do. In the end, like that little tree, they fall over.

Becoming Dispensable

A key to effective parenting is for a parent to increasingly make himself dispensable to his children. That will help them learn to make their own choices and use their own powers. When parents are too involved in their children's problems, the children never have a chance to become responsible. The parents are doing it all for them.

Much better is for the parent to encourage, but not become directly involved. As the parent withdraws from involvement in the child's problems, the child will feel the pressure to feel responsible—and will react accordingly.

Twelve-year-old Chad has a paper route—and it's giving his mom fits. Chad is supposed to get up at six so he can get his papers all delivered before school starts. But he's gotten into a bad habit: when mom calls him to get up, he moans and rolls over. His feet don't hit the floor until the fourth or fifth call. Then he pokes and pokes. Half the time mom ends up driving him on his route. And crabs at him all the way there and back.

That's destructive involvement. Mom should try something new, namely, withdrawing herself from Chad's job. She buys him an alarm clock and explains the new rules:

1. Chad gets himself up and off on his route.

2. If he's late getting off, he'll probably be late for school. If he's late for school, he'll have to suffer the consequences.

3. If he's so late his customers complain, he may lose his job. Then he'll have to find his spare money somewhere else—but it won't come from mom and dad.

The first couple of weeks are rough going. Chad *likes* being dependent. It's easier than being responsible. He has to go see the principal at school for being late four days in a row. A couple of customers call and complain.

But Chad wants to keep the job, and he doesn't want to have problems at school. By the end of the second week he's begun to establish a pattern of responsibility. It's a pattern that will benefit him throughout his life.

And all mom had to do was withdraw involvement and let Chad be responsible for his paper route.

What's a Parent to Do?

As long as a parent does the child's jobs for him, the child will never learn to be responsible. And with a baby that's fine—babies shouldn't be expected to do much for themselves. But as a child grows older and older he grows more and more capable of being responsible. That's when the parent needs to wean him of his dependency and help him learn to do things on his own.

It's easy to let a child lean. It often comes so naturally—the child needs help and you're there, with the ability to provide it. But we need to resist our natural urges. Let the child stand on his own two feet as he grows. It won't happen all at once. But gradually he'll be able to strike out on his own, little by little. And make his parent dispensable!

Children who are allowed to lean on their parents too much become too dependent. And dependency and responsibility rarely go together.

Do This or You'll Regret It

Kids are great copy cats. They like to do the things they see their parents do.

A man and his son were shopping in a grocery store. The man was talking to one of the clerks—and as he talked, he continually reached into a bin of nuts and helped himself to the peanuts. The man's little boy watched him for a while, then reached into the bin to get a nut for himself. The man instantly slapped the boy's hand.

"We don't take things we haven't paid for," he said. "That's stealing."

Kids are wonderful copy cats. They'll act like us whether we say "Simon Says" or not. They look like their parents, they talk like their parents, they want to be like their parents—and so they act like it.

If a parent wants his child to be responsible, he should act responsibly himself. Kids invariably follow models. The models (usually their parents) help them know what they should act like, how they should be. Kids don't know, of course, whether or not their model is a good one. They only know what they see—and that's what they want to become.

This principle has been so fully recognized that it has made its way into the cliches of our language:

- Practice what you preach.

- Do as I say, not as I do. (This one never works.)

- Actions speak louder than words.

What's a Parent to Do?

Before a parent can truly raise a responsible child, the parent must himself be responsible. And we can turn that statement around, and it will also be true: Parents who provide a good example of being responsible usually find it fairly easy to get their kids to be responsible as well. In fact, a child will generally develop responsibility in direct proportion to the amount of responsible behavior he sees around him.

This idea has a very practical application, though it's easier to say than to do. Whenever our children are doing something we don't like, whenever they are being irresponsible in one way or another, we need to analyze *ourselves* first. As yourself these questions:

What is my real attitude toward this behavior?

Why do I consider the child as irresponsible?

What is my own behavior—am I setting a good example?

If my model isn't a good one, what do I need to do to change?

How do we get our children to change and do better? An important first step is to change and do better ourselves! This solution, of course, isn't the easiest one. But it's far and away the most effective.

Summary

Why This Book Can Make a Difference
Responsibility is the magic wand that can help children be everything they should be.

Why Nagging Doesn't Teach Responsibility
In helping children learn to be responsible, it works best to emphasize the positive and deemphasize the negative.

Why Most Kids Aren't Responsible
If a child isn't taught how to be responsible, he probably won't ever learn.

When to Start Teaching Responsibility
The best time to start is NOW!

How Much Responsibility Do You Give?
Don't give too much or too little: fit the load to the child's back.

A Starting Point to Building Responsibility
In working with your child, begin with his strengths, not his weaknesses.

"You Think Funny!"
A vital element in communicating with our children: see things from their point of view.

The Secret of Unconditional Love
When a child believes his parents truly love him, he is usually more responsive to their teachings.

A No-Fail Way to Make a Child Irresponsible
If a child is given more than he can handle, he'll invariably end up being irresponsible.

If You Rely on This, You're Headed for Trouble!
Children can't be exhorted into much of anything good—yet it's the approach parents most often use.

There's No Excuse for This
Children become more responsible when they learn not to make excuses.

Give 'Em What They Deserve!
Natural and logical consequences help a child learn that he does have to be responsible for his actions.

A Surefire Way of Getting Children Interested
When children are allowed to stretch toward their potential, they tend to develop more responsibility.

Try This and You'll Be Amazed at the Results
When a child gets feedback on how he's doing, he usually starts to do even better.

A Vital Technique That's Often Overlooked
When children learn how to sacrifice, they also learn how to be more responsible.

"I'm Running Out of Patience!"
As a child's patience level rises, so can his level of responsibility.

But MY Kid Never Keeps the Rules!
Here's a key: teach children correct principles, and then let them rule themselves.

An Unavoidable Part of Responsibility
Risk goes hand in hand with learning responsibility. But it's worth it.

Little Things That Help in Teaching Responsibility
The little things in the parent-child relationship can mean a lot.

How a Fence Can Help a Child to Grow
The safer a child feels, the more she'll be able to learn responsibility.

Out of the Rut and into the Groove
How to get a child out of a bad habit-pattern into a good one.

One Way to Increase Your Chances of Raising a Responsible Child
Be sensitive to the needs of each child. Each is unique and special.

A Key Factor to Becoming Responsible

Learning to cope with failure and disappointment is a key to becoming a responsible person.

Helping the Child to Love Himself

Self-esteem can lead to esteem of others—which can lead to greater responsibility.

How to Kill Responsibility Fast!

When parents are inconsistent in what they expect from a child, the child doesn't know what to be responsible to.

Ignoring This Can Undo All Your Good Work

Children learn responsibility from role models, both real and in the media.

When Did You Last Meet a Perfect 10?

Nobody's perfect—and children find it easier to be more responsible when they're not burdened with expectations of perfection.

One of the Easiest Ways to Help a Child Become Responsible

Create circumstances where the child will have to do for herself the things she's capable of doing.

When Children NEVER Seem to Learn

One of the best ways to help a child learn to be responsible is to give him practice with it.

The Great Responsibility Thief

Discouragement almost invariably decreases the ability to be responsible.

How to Figure Out
Where Your Child Stands Now

Before a parent can make progress with a child, he needs to find out how responsible the child is to start with.

How to Get to the Essence of Responsibility

Choices are the essence of responsibility. Demands are the genesis of irresponsibility.

Why "Do It My Way!" Doesn't Work

Parents who dictate not only what a child should do, but how he should do it find themselves with a motivation problem on their hands.

Ten Easy Rules for Raising a Delinquent
44Things a parent should never do.

The Best Thing a Parent Can Do
Perhaps the best thing a parent can ever do for her child is to believe in him.

When Children Don't Finish What They Start
Children who can learn to finish what they start will find it easier to learn to be responsible.

One Important Thing to Remember about Kids
Kids are kids; they're not just small adults. All they can do is act their age.

How to Increase a Child's Desire to Be More Responsible
When a parent explains the whys and wherefores, it helps the child want to be more responsible.

An Important Tip about Teaching Responsibility
Most new responsibilities are best learned by starting small and working up.

How to Use Punishment That Brings Results
Sometimes punishment is the best way to change irresponsible behavior. Here's how to make it work.

You Say Your Kids Won't Do Their Work?
The more kids are encouraged and rewarded for doing the right thing, the more they'll want to do it.

How to Make the Right Things Happen
Extremes in parenting styles are common, but they simply don't work. It's the parent who finds a good middle ground who has the greatest chance of raising a responsible child.

"I Never Get No Respect!"
The more a child respects something, the more he'll act responsibly toward it.

A Way to Make Teaching Responsibility Easier
A good relationship between parent and child makes teaching responsibility much easier.

How to Really Get Children Going
Goals and objectives often help to increase responsibility.

A Way to Get Kids Saying "Yes!"
Letting a child decide what he'll be responsible
for—and how—gets him more involved. And greater
involvement tends to lead to greater responsibility.

The Best Way of All to Teach Responsibility
The more a parent becomes dispensable, the greater
the child's chances of becoming responsible.

Do This or You'll Regret It
If a parent wants his child to be responsible, he should
act responsibly himself.